BERNEY ARMS : PAST & PRESENT

GW00750920

Revised Ed.

Sheila Murphy

This book is dedicated to the memory of my grandparents Henry Bumbury Hewitt and Annie Maria Hewitt.

Front Cover Photograph: Henry Bumbury Hewitt, known locally as 'Yoiton', of Ashtree Farm, Berney Arms taken by the Berney Arms Mill in the 1950's. (Photograph from Peter Allard Collection.)

Back Cover: Front of a hand-made Christmas Card made by Ron Carter and sent to 'Yoiton', circa 1960, depicting the Berney Arms Inn. (Supplied by Stanley and Barbara Hewitt.)

1

Berney Arms : Past and Present.

ISBN 9780957462342

First Edition published 2000
Second Edition published 2001

Published
by
Sheila & Paul Hutchinson
7, Colman Avenue,
Stoke Holy Cross.
Norwich
NR14 8NA
e-mail address:-
sandp@paulsheila.plus.com

Printed
by
Really Useful Print Co. Ltd.
Bessemer Rd.
Norwich.

Berney Arms : Past and Present.

About The Author:

As a baby I lived at Raven Hall, Langley Marshes, on The Island opposite
Berney Arms, for about a year around 1947. I then lived at No. 1 Cottage
Berney Arms with my parents Mr and Mrs Joseph and Ellen Williams, my
younger sister Maureen and younger brother Derek. In 1959 we moved into
Nos 6 and 7 Cottages, Berney Arms, and lived there until we moved in 1963
into Cobholm, Gt. Yarmouth. We were one of the last families living in the
cottages at Berney Arms before they were pulled down.

Acknowledgements:

It has been a great pleasure to meet up with many people who have
lived or worked at Berney Arms, having been warmly welcomed into their
homes for a good old yarn about how it once was. I wish to thank them all.
I wish to express many thanks to the following people and organizations
for their help in providing valuable information and permission to reproduce
photographs, information and tales for this Book:-
Mr Peter Allard. Mr Andrew Barton. Mr John Berney. Mr Mike Browne. Mr
Roy Carr. Mr Jack Carter. Mr Ron Carter. Mr Rod Clark. Mr Sidney Gibbs. Dr.
Ian G. Gray. Mr & Mrs Trevor and Carol Goreham. Mrs Dorothy Hanton. Mr &
Mrs Stanley and Barbara Hewitt. Mr Ernest Hewitt. Mr Arnold Hewitt. Mr
Kavan Hunt. Ms. Amanda Jaques of The Norfolk Windmills Trust. Mr & Mrs
Bob & Violet Mace. Mr Ivan Mace. Mr Reginald Mathews. Mr David Pyett .Mr
Keith Rackham. Mr Edward Roberts. Mr Arthur C. Smith. Mrs Linda Smith. Mr
Derek Williams. Mr Joseph Williams. Mrs Carol Williams. Eastern Daily Press.
Eastern Evening News. Great Yarmouth Mercury. Norfolk Records Office.

Special thanks go to Paul Hutchinson for all his encouragement, help,
typing and preparing the book layout.

Disclaimer:-
Much of the information herein is from people's memories and therefore may
contain some errors as often people's memories are less accurate than they
believe. I have tried to check the accuracy but I apologise for any errors that may
be present, and I cannot accept responsibility for the consequences of any errors
and omissions.

Berney Arms : Past and Present.

INTRODUCTION

This revised edition has the 1911 census information, some alterations to bring it up to date, and some additional information added. The early editions have been out of print and unavailable since 2001 and I have been asked for the book many times as people love to go for walks along the Wherryman's Way to Berney Arms to have a meal or a drink at the Berney inn or to visit the windmill or go bird watching.

The RSPB bought Ashtree Farm in the 1980s and Ralph Loughlin was a warden there from the start. He was not an office person but very 'hands on', fixing gates, working on the marshes and helping people understand the wild life. Sadly he passed away in November 2015. He is sadly missed by his family, friends and colleagues.

INTRODUCTION TO THE FIRST EDITION

I am writing this little book about Berney Arms as there is only Berney Arms Inn, Ashtree Farm, now owned by the R.S.P.B., and the Berney High Mill there today, but going back through the years it was a hamlet and a hive of activity. As there is no book about Berney Arms I thought I would give it a go.

Berney Arms lies on the north bank of the river Yare, in the parish of Reedham in the county of Norfolk. Travelling along the river, Ashtree Farm House is situated about four miles from the Reedham swing bridge and almost five miles from Great Yarmouth's Haven Bridge. By rail Berney Arms Halt is a little under four miles from Reedham station and a little over five miles from Yarmouth's Vauxhall Station. There are no proper public roadways to and from Berney Arms, and it can only be reached by rail, river, or on foot across the marshes, walking along the old right of way known as 'Weaver's Way', or walking along the river wall.

When I lived at Berney Arms back in the late 1940's and through to the early 1960's there were more buildings. Walking along the river wall from Seven Mile House towards Yarmouth the first buildings you would reach were a row of four cottages, known then as 1 to 4 Cottages, continuing along the 'strip' you came to Ashtree Farm. Walking further along the river wall there was the electric pump and the Berney Arms Windmill, and then, past what was left of the cement works foundations and rubble, you came to the Bungalow. Beyond that was another building built as semi-detached cottages and known as 6 and 7 Cottages. A bit further along was the Berney Arms Inn and beyond that on Breydon Water was the Breydon Pump followed by Lockgate Mill and a marsh house. All of these buildings were near the river and it was a good walk across the marshes to the station where another building existed. This was the station houses and was constructed as two dwellings, one of which had a waiting room, which was also used as a post office. A wooden railway signal box was also close by.

Excluding Seven Mile house, Lockgate Mill marsh house, and the Langley Detached Ravenhall which were not part of the Berney Arms hamlet, there was at one time eleven dwellings and families living at Berney Arms, all making a living in some way.

In earlier times there was also another mill, Tuck's Mill, located on the Reedham side of 1 to 4 Cottages and a Brickworks located behind these cottages.

Figure 1 shows an early sketch map of the area with the location of the buildings.

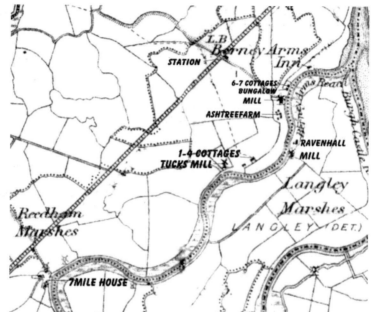

Figure 1 Ordnance Survey Map from circa 1913 of Berney Arms Hamlet and Seven-Mile Reedham with buildings highlighted.

SEVEN MILE HOUSE. (TG445035)

Seven Mile House, Reedham is on the outskirts of Berney Arms. It was given this name because it is approximately 7 miles from Yarmouth along the river. It was marked on Faden's Map 1797 as 'Lower Seven Mile House'. It is a marsh house and farm and there are three derelict drainage windmills close by known today as Polkey's mill, Cadge's mill and the North mill. Previously there had also been two steam pumps used for draining the marshes and then a diesel pump, and now an electric pump is used. There was also another dwelling adjacent to Polkeys mill which was occupied by the Thaxter family during the nineteenth century and was demolished in the 1950s.

Nearby there are three railway cottages which are now derelict and overgrown.

5

Berney Arms : Past and Present.

Many generations of the Burgess family lived at Seven Mile house according to the censuses, and right up till about 1942. Fred Hewitt occupied the house for a few years after Fred Burgess left, and in 1945 it was occupied by the Mace family. Figure 2 shows Reggie Mace photographed at Seven Mile House.

Seven Mile house, according to Ivan Mace, had two large living rooms, a large kitchen, a large pantry, and five bedrooms. There was once a cowshed in which they had an electric generator. When they first went there the house was larger than shown in the photograph and on the left of the photograph, where the water buts are, there was more structure but it was falling down and was demolished.

Figure 2. Mr Reggie Mace with Seven Mile House in the background on the left of the photograph, circa 1980. Photograph supplied by Ivan Mace.

In the cowshed roof there were some glass panels and in 1976, during the hot summer, the hay in the cowshed caught fire and the cowshed was destroyed. They had four calves in there and these too were lost in the fire. Fire engines came to put the fire out and about two hours after they had gone the fire flared up again and they had to return.

Reggie Mace originally came from Reedham. He left school aged 12, after his father died, and went to live at Ashtree Farm working for William Hewitt, nicknamed 'The King' or 'King Billy'. Reggie married Blanche Hewitt, one of King Billy's grand-daughters, and Yoiton's sister. They had nine children, most of them when they lived at the Bungalow at Berney Arms. They moved to Seven Mile on 10th. March 1945 where Reggie became the marshman. Although Blanche died in 1968 Reggie stayed at Seven Mile House till about 1985. Ivan Mace recalls that they had their groceries from the co-op in Yarmouth, they were delivered by train to Reedham, and they had to cycle along the railway track to Reedham to collect them. The Reedham postman delivered their mail. He, too, cycled down the railtracks.

When the electric pump was built in the early 1980's, the Drainage Board also made a concrete road from Wickhampton to Seven Mile for easier access.

When we lived at Berney Arms we had our Christmas goose from Reggie Mace. Our father, Joseph Williams, would walk to Seven Mile house to collect it. He would put the goose, still alive, in a sack, sling it over his shoulder, and carry it home to Berney Arms. The goose would be struggling and father would have many a nip on his backside before he got home to Berney. Bob Mace, one of Reggie's sons, recalls that when he lived at the Station cottages at Berney he too used to walk to Seven Mile to collect his Christmas goose. He would kill the goose before setting off back to Berney and would pluck it as he walked home.

Figure 3. Queen of the Broads sailing past Seven Mile House in the 1950's. Photograph supplied by Ivan Mace. This boat was built in 1889 by Thomas Bradley, founder of Yarmouth and Gorleston Steamboat Company. It made trips from Yarmouth along the Yare turning after Seven Mile House to return. She was broken up in 1976.

Berney Arms : Past and Present.

DRAINAGE MILLS AT SEVEN MILE.

Polkey's Mill. (TG445035)

This mill, which stands only a few yards from Seven Mile House, was marked on Faden's map of 1797 and on all subsequent maps. It has also been known as Seven Mile Mill and the current name is thought to be after a marshman 'Polkey' Thaxter who worked the mill for many years. The present mill was probably built between 1840 and 1880. It drove a scoopwheel and on the floodgate it has inscribed 'Barnes'. This probably refers to R. Barnes, a millwright of Southtown, Great Yarmouth who was active in the 1860's through to the early 1880's.

It was a black tarred tower mill which had patent sails, an eight-bladed fantail and a boat-shaped cap. The mill last worked about 1941. The mill has been renovated in recent years by the Norfolk Windmill Trust with a new cap and sails. Figure 5 shows the mill as it was in 1899 in working condition.
An old cradle hoist, which was used for doing repairs to the mills, was still at this old mill when the Mace family were at Seven Mile House.

Figure 4. The riverboard repairing the river wall at Seven Mile after the 1953 floods. Polkey's mill and the Steam pump chimney are in the background and Seven Mile house is on the left. Alan Brackenbury is standing on the wherry, and in the crowd are, on the far right, Fred Burgess, then to his left, Ivan Mace, and then Reggie Mace. The man at the left of the foreground carrying the sandbag is young Jack Farrow. Courtesy of E.D.P.

Seven Mile Steam Mill. (TG446035)

This was built in about 1880, the inscription reads 'J.W.R. 1880', and refers to J.W.

8

Rose of Reedham Hall. This drove a turbine pump by R. Barnes of Southtown, Great Yarmouth. It was built to replace an earlier steam drainage mill at TG447036 and was last worked in 1941 when the diesel plant took over. The interior walls of the building were covered in pine panelling and the floors were black and white tiles. Much of the machinery of the old mill was sold in the 1960's as scrap metal.

The tall chimney stack, which can be seen on the right of figure 5 blew down in 1976 during the winter gales. Most of the buildings of this old steam mill are still in existence, and the building has been renovated in recent years to be used as a visitor attraction.

North Mill. (TG443036)

This was not shown on Faden's, Wyand's, or Bryant's maps and first appears on the O.S. map of 1837, so it was probably built between about 1825 to 1840. It was probably built as a 'helper' mill to assist the water from the Seven Mile Level to the other mills alongside the river. The mill was a small tower mill and was probably last used around 1904. It was derelict when Ivan Mace lived at Seven Mile House in the late 1940's, and it was in much the same state as it is now, back in 1904 according to information provided by 'Yoiton' to Peter Allard.

Cadge's Mill. (TG446036)

This was known as Cadge's or Kedge's Mill. It was marked on Faden's and Bryant's map, but the current mill was probably built about 1880. 'Yoiton' told Peter Allard that when it was first built it had buckets attached to the scoopwheel, but this was not very successful. The scoopwheel was inside the mill. This was a tarred brick tower mill with two doors, patent sails, an 8 bladed fantail and a typical boat shaped cap. The scoopwheel was sixteen feet in diameter and the paddles 14 inches wide. It was last worked in 1941 and Ivan Mace recalls that the sails of this mill were removed and taken

Figure 5. Polkey's Mill in 1899, with the steam mill on the right edge. Photograph from Peter Allard collection.

9

away to be put onto another mill elsewhere. Figure 7 shows the mill in full working order in the mid 1930's, and figure 6 shows Reggie Hewitt on the sails probably when the sails were being removed around 1941. The hole in the wall of the tower, seen in figure 6 above and to the left of the door, was the chimney. This mill had a fire inside.

The controls for the new electric pump were installed in this mill.

**Figure 6. Reggie Hewitt working on the sails of Cadge's mill.
Photograph supplied by Linda Smith.**

Seven Mile Diesel Pump. (TG447036)

This was built in 1941 and had 3 single cylinder Ruston and Hornsby engines supplied new in 1941 by William Foster & Co. Lincolnshire. Two engines power the centrifugal pumps marked Gwynnes, and the other, a starting engine with 2 flywheels, drives a Ruston and Hornsby air compressor and a suction priming pump. It was last used in the early 1980's and was superseded by an electric pump. After the 1953 floods Reggie Mace had this pump working continuously for 3 days. It is now in the care of the Norfolk Windmills Trust and following alterations to the river wall it was recently moved closer to Polkeys Mill.

Seven Mile Steam Mill. (TG 447036)

This was the predecessor of the above steam mill and lay to the east of the diesel plant. It was not marked on any maps and was probably built around 1850's and last used in the 1880's. A few brick remains were visible showing sluice bay and housing for a scoopwheel, but following the alterations to the River Wall in recent years there is now no signs left of its existence.

Figure 7. Cadge's Mill in the mid-1930's. Photograph from Peter Allard collection.

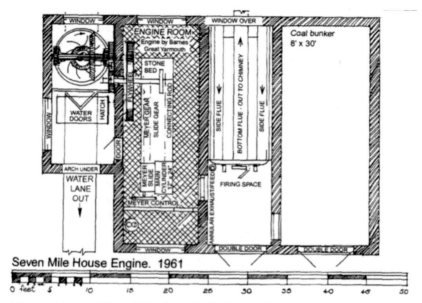

Figure 8. Floor Plan of the Seven Mile Steam Pump engine house at TG446035 drawn by A. J, Ward.

Figure 9. Diesel Pump House at Seven Mile by the River Wall in 2000 before it was moved.

Berney Arms : Past and Present.

Figure 10. Tuck's Mill with in the background cottages 1 to 4 shown on the right and Ashtreee Farm farmhouse on the left .
Photograph supplied by Peter Allard

This was a drainage mill, and though not marked on Faden's Map of 1797, it did appear on Wyand's Map of 1823, and on Bryant's Map of 1826, where it was called Berney's Mill. It was also shown on Ordnance Survey Maps of 1835-

13

37, 1884, 1904, 1913 and 1926 were it was shown as a drainage windpump.

Figure 10 shows a photograph of Tuck's Mill with 1-4 Cottages in the background on the right hand side and Ashtree Farmhouse on the left. It is possible that it may have been rebuilt at some stage in the late nineteenth century and may not be the original mill which was built sometime before 1823.

The mill was a brick tower mill of average height and tarred. It carried four patent sails which turned anti-clockwise into the wind. These were double shuttered with 9 bays, with 3 shutters in each bay and a total of 54 shutters per sail. The mill had a boat-shaped cap with no gallery and carried an 8-bladed fantail. The sails were adjusted with a chain guide pole with a Y-wheel. It drove a large scoop wheel, but no details of size are available.

Figure 11. The Polly M heading towards Reedham, photographed September 1948 from Langley Detached Mill, showing on the far right cottages 1 to 4 and towards the centre the brick tower remains of Tuck's Mill. Photograph supplied by Rod Clark.

It was known as Tuck's Mill according to 'Yoiton', Henry Hewitt, Mr Bob Mace, Mr Joseph Williams, and Mr Ernest Hewitt, however, we have not found in the censuses, or in conversations, any evidence of a Mr Tuck. It is, however, likely that it was named after a marshman or a landowner or perhaps even someone's nickname.

Tuck's mill was the responsibility of Mr Fred Burgess of Seven Mile House in the 1930's, and he paid Jack Farrow, who lived at No.1 Cottage, Berney Arms near the 'strip' to operate the drainage mill.

There are a variety of tales of how the mill was damaged putting it out of action in 1941. One of them as told to Peter Allard by 'Yoiton', is that on 26th. April a bomb landed on the piece of land near the riverbank known to the locals as the 'strip'. Shortly afterwards during a westerly gale the four sails were caught by the wind from behind and a fire started in the cap destroying the cap and the sails. Jack Farrow was an elderly man with bad legs and was unable the put out the fire. Bob Mace provided me with a similar account: 'The sails were caught by the wind from behind and because the brake had not been fully applied they began to turn backwards. The friction started the fire destroying the cap and the sails. The burning sails looked like a Catherine wheel. The mill was not hit by a bomb but bombs were dropped on the strip once the mill was alight'.

The brick shell stood for several years until around 1950-51 when Reginald Matthews who owned the Berney Inn at the time bought the shell for £100, dismantled the tower brick by brick, and used the bricks to build a septic tank at the inn and make other repairs to the inn.

The footings of Tuck's Mill were uncovered in 1999 but following the alterations to the river wall and the dykes there is now no visible evidence of its existence.

COTTAGES 1 TO 4.(TG462044)

These terraced cottages, known to the locals as the 'Barracks', were built of red brick and tiled roof. They were probably built for the families working at the brickworks which were located at the field at the back of the cottages. The brickground was shown on the 1823 map and the cottages were mentioned in a newspaper advert in 1828 in the Norfolk Chronicle when the Cement Works were to be let. The advert is shown later in the section on the cement works. The cottages are believed to have been built sometime before 1823.

No. 1 Cottage is where dad and mum, Joseph {nicknamed 'Paddy'} and Ellen {nicknamed 'Nibby'} Williams, lived until 1959 with me and younger sister and brother, Maureen and Derek.

When we lived here there was a dyke around these cottages and a small wooden bridge across the dyke on the river wall side of the cottages. There was a ligger (*a plank bridge over a dyke*) going across the dyke on the side to Tuck's mill and another at the back of the cottages near the toilets leading to the marsh field where the brickworks had once stood. At one time there was also a cowshed on this marsh. Each cottage had a large garden and at no 4 there was a beautiful apple tree and a plum tree. The gardens were always kept neat and tidy.

Dad was a cowman and worked for 'Yoiton' and at one time he had two pigs called Porky and Slim. Later he worked for the riverboard.

There was no gas or electricity and we used Mantel lamps, oil lamps and candles for our lighting. The cooking was done with a coal fire cooking range. We had no controls on the oven and you had to judge how hot your oven was.

Berney Arms : Past and Present.

Running water from a tap was only a dream, the water we had came from the roof, collected in the guttering and taken down the drainpipe into a tank. An old sock on the downpipe was the only filter. A bucket of water was always placed on the floor or the table ready in the kitchen for filling the kettle to boil water for tea and washing etc. In the winter time the water in the bucket would freeze as it was so cold indoors and we would have to break the ice to use the water.

We did not have a bath, just strip washes.

Clothes were washed in a copper with a fire underneath. It would be filled up by hand with buckets of water from the barrel outside and emptied by hand with a handcup or scoop. To do the ironing a flat iron was used. It was heated up in the fire and placed into an iron-shoe.

The toilet was down the back garden. It was built of brick and had a long bench with a hole in it, and a bucket placed underneath. The bucket was emptied regularly and the rhubarb grew "bew'ful". Figure 13 shows Eliza Hewitt near the toilets at no 2 cottage.

All our refuse was buried at the bottom of the garden.

Figure 12. Cottages 1 to 4, called the 'Barracks', in the 1950s.
Photograph supplied by David Pyett.

Each cottage had two bedrooms and an attic. The attics had a window facing the river. Downstairs was a living room, kitchen, with a copper, and a dinning room. In no 1 we had a walk-in larder with long marble slabs and we believed this was once a dairy.

Mondays were grocery-box days. Our parents would go into Yarmouth to Mr Downing, then on Howard Street, and take their grocery book with the grocery list written in it. Mr Downing would deliver the grocery box to the Yarmouth railway station in his van, and the train would drop the grocery box off at Berney Arms station where our father would collect it either on foot or with a horse and cart. Just before Christmas each year we would all take a trip to

Yarmouth to fetch a real Christmas tree from the market.

When I came of school age I should have gone to Reedham school but the train times had been changed so badly that I would have had to wait from 4:00 till 5:30 for a train to get back to Berney Arms after school. Walking across the muddy winter marshes in the pitch dark was not thought suitable for a young child, and after long negotiations I was allowed to go to school at Gt. Yarmouth. My younger sister and brother did the same when they started school.

I remember when brother Derek was born, July 1952: a misty morning sitting outside with sister Maureen. Our father in the early hours of the morning had to go for help at the old Berney Arms inn and Mrs Muriel Forster came to help with the delivery as Nurse Jackson of Reedham could not come immediately as she had two births at Reedham to attend first.

Pushing a pram across a single ligger must have been very difficult, balancing the pram on two wheels. There was not many double liggers.

When the floods came in 1953 everywhere around the marshes was heavily flooded but we did not get any water indoors. I do, however, vaguely remember spending some time in the attic in case the house became flooded.

In the mid-1950's the Rev. Lionel Lawrence came down from Reedham on Saturday afternoons and gave bible classes for the children in the front room of the east station cottage.

Figure 13. Eliza Hewitt with grand-daughter Patricia near the toilet at number 2 cottage on the strip, circa 1938. Photograph supplied by Violet Mace.

We were the last family to live in these cottages and when 2 to 4 became empty our father used all of the gardens. We moved out in 1959 and moved to 6 & 7 cottages.

These cottages were pulled down shortly afterwards by Stanley Hewitt and Alan Brackenbury and the brick rubble was used to fill in the ruts, caused by cartwheels, on the tracks across the marshes. Maurice Hanton and Joseph Williams carried the brick rubble by horse and cart across the marshes to the rutted tracks.

Along the strip from the 'Barracks', at a spot near the bend, at a certain time of the year you would sometimes hear a faint clanking noise. It would get louder as if something was approaching and moving towards the dyke nearby. You would feel the ground vibrate and a breeze go past. There was never any sign of anything that could make this noise. Another ghostly story is that there was a crinoline lady that appeared by the big Arch gate and was seen by several people.

SOME OCCUPANTS OF 1 TO 4 COTTAGES ON THE STRIP.

NAMES	APPROX. DATES	NOTES
William & Harriet Hewitt and family. (Ernest Norman, Billy, Betty & Sid)	1920s	Harriet was sister to Yoiton
Cathy Skyoles	1940's	WW11 evacuee, stepsister to Nora Hewitt at the farmhouse.
Jack and Florrie Farrow & Norah, Lilly, Bob & Jack	c. 1920 to early 1940's	At no.1, Son Bob died in WW2. They moved to railway cottages at 7 Mile. Son Jack moved to Caister and biked every day to 7 Mile to work..
Ernest Hewit (& wife Lily & son Tony)	1920's & early 1930's	No.2 & then no. 3. Left Berney Arms in.1935.
Eliza Hewitt	late 1920's & 1930's	At no.2 then moved to station cottages.
Fred High and Millie (nee Hewitt) & family	mid 1940's to 1946	No.1. Moved to the Island.
Aubrey Appleton	1940's	No.2. Moved to Bungalow
Joseph & Ellen Williams & family	1946 & 1948 to 1959	No.1/ moved to 6/7 Berney Arms in 1959.
Billy & Elsie Bailey	to 1947	No.2. Billy died 1947.
Albert Hewitt & daughter Violet	1930's to 1947	No.3 & moved to station 1947.
Jack French & family	1947 to 1949	No.3 . Then moved to Lockgate.
Dick French & family	till 1953	No.2.
'Long' Jimmy & 'Lady' Rose Hewitt	1920's till early 1950's	No.4. She kept chickens, their son Arthur James died in WW2.
Sailing Club Members	1953 to 1958	No. 2.
Easter family	to 1957	No.4 .

18

Berney Arms : Past and Present.

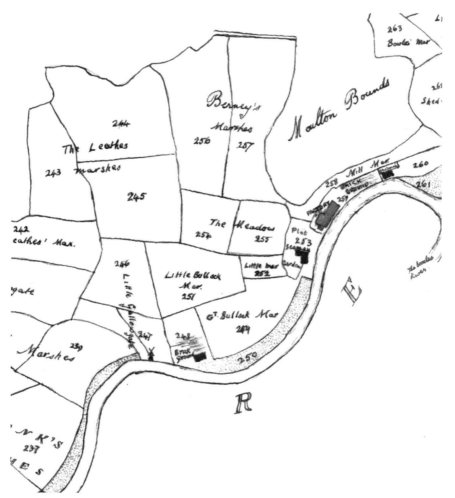

Figure 14. Benjamin Wyand Map of 1823 showing location of the brick grounds, cement works and Tucks Mill.

BRICKWORKS. (TG462044)

Brickworks once existed on the field at the back of 1-4 Cottages and were shown on Wyand's Map of 1823 as 'brick grounds'; as 'kilns' on Bryant's map of 1826; as 'Brickyard' on the Ordnance Survey Map of 1835, and as 'Old Brick Yard' in 1890. Part of Wyand's map of Reedham is reproduced in figure 14 and shows the location of the brickworks. Another brickground is also shown located between the cement works and the public house on this map.

More information on the brickworks is given in the section on the Cement Works.

19

Berney Arms : Past and Present.

ASHTREE FARMHOUSE.(TG464048)

Figure 15. William Hewitt, known as 'King Billy' or 'The King', circa 1918. Photograph supplied by Violet Mace.

The east part of Ashtree Farmhouse is believed to have been built during 1750 to 1752. The west part, which housed a chapel on the ground floor, was built sometime later. It is a redbrick building with a thatched roof and it has been suggested that originally it was built as a former manor house for some of the Berney family who were large landowners in Reedham. Faden's map of 1797 shows a house at this location labelled '5 Mile House', it was probably given this name because it was five miles from Yarmouth by river. On the Ordnance Survey maps of 1883, 1890 and through to 1996 it was called Ashtree Farm, a name it still has today.

There was no electricity at the farmhouse until about 1949 when electricity was laid on from the new electric Pump.

It had running water from a spring in the big yard and also had water from the roof guttering going into a tank. The sewage was buried in the garden.

There were various outbuildings, cowsheds, cart sheds and a hay-yard in the 1950's

The censuses show that different families have occupied the farmhouse and that a John Burgess, marshman, occupied the farmhouse during the period from 1868 to 1883 according to Harrod's and White's Directories.

Figure 16. Jimmy Hewitt nicknamed 'Wesmacot' on the left. Photograph supplied by Linda Smith.

The Hewitt family first appeared as the occupants in the 1891 census when William Hewitt, ('King Billy'), was listed as the marshman at the farmhouse. The Hewitt family must have taken over some time between 1883 and 1891. William Hewitt had previously been a marshman on the island opposite and was in a marsh house on the Chedgrave level in the 1881 census. In William's day it was very hard work at the mills, repairing and painting the sails. William would ride the sails down creeping out until the sails of the mill turned with his weight, and he would ride them down to the ground.

William Hewitt, could neither read nor write. He had a weird way of writing, it looked like squares, triangles and marks. A well known tale is that when the top of Langley mill blew off in a storm he did an estimate for mending it against another millwright, who unlike William, could read and write. His estimate was only two shillings and sixpence different. William was not only a marshman but a millwright and a wheelwright also. He lived to a ripe old age of about 87 and died in 1928. A studio portrait photograph of William Hewitt is shown in figure 15.

Figure 17. Reggie Hewitt as a boy at Ashtree Farm. Note the initials 'W H' on the back wall, probably referring to William Hewitt.
Photograph supplied by Linda Smith

One of William's many sons, James David Hewitt, (nicknamed 'Wesmacot'), shown in figure 16, took over as the marshman and lived at Ashtree farm with his wife Eunice Georgina. Their son Reggie, shown in figure 17, married Norah, and they lived in one part of the farmhouse which later became known as 'Norahs End'. Reggie became a carpenter, millwright and wheelwright and made all of his furniture. He used one of the outbuildings as his carpenters shop.

'Yoiton', Henry Hewitt, took over as marshman at Ashtree farm in 1946 when his uncle, 'Wesmacot', left to go to Wickhampton. 'Yoiton' lived here with his wife Annie Maria and son Stanley ('Sonny'); my mother Ellen Marie ('Nibby') and her sister Ruth Margaret ('Pinny') having both married during the war years. Stanley married Barbara in 1949 and moved to Raven Hall on the Island leaving 'Yoiton' and Annie at Ashtree farm on their own.

When we were children and went to visit our grandparents at Ashtree farm we were never allowed to go upstairs in the west part of the house because it was in need of repair. There was a story told that it was haunted up there and that, years ago two brothers had a sword fight and one was killed. His blood was on the floorboards and no matter how often it was cleaned the bloodstains kept returning! Another story is that a lady dressed in black would appear in the chapel.

'Yoiton' had a teak boat called 'Quick Return' which was hit by a cruiser in 1949 and sank. The wreck is believed to be there still at the quayside at Ashtree Farm. The wherry 'Lady Violet', built many years ago at Yarmouth and of 27 tons, registered at Loddon, and last owned by Case and Steward lay adjacent to Ashtree farm for a few years. 'Yoiton', when he was the marshman requested the River Board to remove it and they took her across to Burgh Castle where she was beached, half full of water and completely rotten from bow to stern.

Figure 18. Eunice and Norah Hewitt, wives of Jimmy and Reggie, at Ashtree farm. Photograph supplied by Linda Smith

When 'Yoiton' retired in the autumn of 1962 he and Annie moved to Cobholm, Great Yarmouth, and Stanley and Barbara, and family, moved into Ashtree farm.

Figure 21 shows Henry and Annie at the door of Ashtree farm.

Accor-ding to Stanley and Barbara Hewitt, when they lived here in the 1960's the farmhouse had six bedrooms, a large living room, another smaller living room, a large kitchen, a back porch and a coal cellar. During their time here a bathroom was installed.

Figure 19 shows the farmhouse as it was in 1960 and in 1999.

Ashtree Farm and some of the marshes (366 acres) were bought from Mr Berney by the RSPB in 1986, sadly bringing an end to the traditional marshman at Berney Arms. The RSPB no longer drain some of the marshes, in order to attract the wading birds such as the mallards, geese, plover and widgeon.

The farmhouse was renovated by the RSPB in 1989. They spent about £220,000, gutted the whole building, added an extension to the north wing, and rebuilt the west part completely.

Berney Arms : Past and Present.

The building contractors were Juby Brothers and the thatch repairs were done by Derek Rowe. The foreman on site was Mr Roy Carr. He recalls that the original foundation at the west end of the farmhouse was old flints and it had to be dug out to put new footings in. When they were working on the north end of the building all of the windows were removed, and when the winds got up and caused turbulence inside the building the whole building swayed. Roy estimated the building swayed by as much as two inches. Their answer to this was to replace the windows as quickly as possible. During his lunch breaks and after work Roy would go eel fishing in a dyke close by the farmhouse. One day he caught sixty pounds of eels in three

Figure 19. Top: Ashtree Farm with 'Yoiton' about 1960. First published in East Anglia Life Magazine, January 1963. Bottom: Ashtree Farmhouse in 1999, after renovation, now the property of the RSPB.

pair of Fyke nets.

Figure 20 shows the farmhouse at the time of rebuilding. It was at this west end where the chapel had been, and a font was still there when the renovations started. The tiles from the chapel floor were taken up and reused in another part of the house. The farmhouse has been made into three dwellings for use by the RSPB people who work there. The rainwater is still collected from the roof and goes into containers and is pumped into tanks and is used for domestic purposes. The spring water is considered to be too saline, full of iron and is only used for flushing the toilets. The spent water goes into septic tanks and soakaways. They also improved the tracks and it is easier for travel by motor vehicle though there are still no proper roads.

Berney Arms : Past and Present.

Figure 20. Three views of Ashtree farmhouse during the renovations photographed in November 1989.

Photographs supplied by Peter Allard.

In recent years, from 2002, the west part has been let to, and occupied by Mr Frank Futter.

'YOITON', HENRY BUMBURY HEWITT.

'Harry is one of the true gentlemen of the world, a man who can rightly be called the salt of the earth. He is always ready to help anyone and asks no reward except a greeting when you see him next, or, if you have them a couple of pound of eels.' Ron Carter 1958.

Henry was Norfolk bred and born and spoke with a hint of a stutter in a broad Norfolk dialect, though he did not stutter when speaking on the radio.

He was born at the east Station cottage, Berney Arms at 2 o'clock on the morning of July 9th 1891. He was one of thirteen children of Eliza Francis and Thomas Edward Hewitt. Emma Hewitt, his aunt, ran a nursery school in the parlour of the Bungalow and Henry and the other children went there before going to school at Reedham by train.

Henry was often called by his nickname 'Yoiton' but my nanny, Annie Maria, always referred to him as Harry. He got his nickname when he was a young boy of about six when, after he had been looking at a litter of white pigs, he said they are all 'Yoitons' meaning they were white ones. No one has been able to explain why he was given the middle name of Bumbury.

24

Berney Arms : Past and Present.

'Yoiton' and his brothers were jokers and once played a joke on their grandfather after he had bought a brown horse. When grandfather left them they painted the horse with whitewash and it looked a dappled colour. When grandfather returned all he could say was 'Them boys again!'

'Yoiton' left school at the age of twelve and went to work for Mr Henry Bailey at his cloth sail mill, Baileys Mill (TG448097), near the river Bure. Shortly afterwards he went to work for Mr Goffin. He was paid two shillings once a fortnight and each time he was paid he went home to Berney Arms to visit the family. His brothers and sisters would have some of his money to buy sweets and have a party.

Figure 21. Henry Bumbury Hewitt and Annie Maria Hewitt at Ashtree Farm.

'Yoiton' became a fisherman joining the East Anglian Fishing Fleet. He kept in touch with his family writing letters and he was a fisherman for about nine years. Figure 22 shows a photograph of 'Yoiton' taken in his mid-twenties, before he grew a moustache and had earrings, when he was at North Shields.

In 1924 he moved into Raven Hall, on Langley Marshes on the Island, and across the river Yare opposite to Ashtree Farm. He was a marshman whose job was to operate the Langley Detached Redbrick drainage mill, and keep a watch on the animals on the marshes, making sure none had fallen into the dykes and counting them. He also had a herd of cows of his own. Russell Mace, who was living at 7 Cottage, Berney Arms, worked for him for a while and would go over to Raven Hall by boat. The milk would be taken to Reedham by boat where it would be picked up from the quayside by lorry. Violet Mace recalls that 'Yoiton' could often be heard singing as he rowed along the river when returning from delivering his milk to Reedham, and after spending some time in a pub there.

'Yoiton' married Annie Maria

Figure22. 'Yoiton', Henry Hewitt when he was a fisherman circa 1918, photographed in North Shields before he had ear rings and a moustache. Photograph supplied by Sidney Gibbs.

Berney Arms : Past and Present.

Baldry, nee Burrage in 1925. She was a widow and had two small daughters, Ellen Marie, nicknamed 'Nibby', and Ruth Margaret, 'Pinny'. In 1926 they had a son Stanley Thomas, nicknamed 'Sonny'. Annie would make butter and cheese and was well known for her mushroom ketchup. She took these to Yarmouth to sell to the Co-op and the market. She also used to make hooky mats from cloth strips and sacking. Their children went to school at Burgh Castle, and would be rowed across from the Island by Henry. On Mayday and the school sports days Henry and Annie would take bags of sweets for the school children.

At one time during the war years, a story is told that 'Yoiton' was in his motorboat on Breydon Water and it began hailing. 'Yoiton' was scared and thew himself to the bottom of the boat thinking he was being shot at by the Germans.

In 1946 'Yoiton' moved to Ashtree Farm with his wife and son. Here he was the marshman and he kept his own cows, some pigs, chickens and a few dogs.

When a flock of starlings flew over 'Yoiton' would shoot at them with his shotgun and kill about sixty. He would pluck and clean them and Annie would make Starling Pie. Jugged hare was another cheap meal on the menu. Dumplings as big as cauliflowers, enjoyed hot or cold with jam or treacle, and eels, which usually came from Jack and Ron Carter, were some of his favourites. 'Yoiton' enjoyed cooking the eels himself. He also enjoyed a raw egg in his cup of tea each morning.

Henry bought a boathouse which his wife Annie painted out. She put up some curtains which she had made. Sometimes my brother, sister, and cousins and I would go there with nanny for our Sunday tea.

A marshman's job was hard work, working all year round in all weathers. In the winter time the gates would be fixed and the drainage dykes would be cleaned, getting all of the weed and reeds out. They used long handled scythes to cut the reed and weed from the dykes, and a meg was used to drag out the cut debris. The meg was like a scythe but had an angled piece to slide the reed onto the hook so it could be pulled out easily. Some would use a long handled fork instead. The dykes would be cleaned so that the water could drain away properly. The pumping would start in the late winter or spring, and until 1949 this would be done by the Berney Arms drainage windmill, but times have changed and it is now done by the electric pump. 'Yoiton' and fellow marshmen had their own levels to look after and some days they would be pumping from early morning going on till late into the night. 'Yoiton' told the tale that on one occasion he had the windmill working continuously for 62 hours to pump the marshes which had become flooded during an earlier spell when there had been no wind to turn the sails.

In the spring and summer the marshes would be let for cattle to graze on. 'Yioton' and fellow marshmen would be paid so much a head to keep a watch on the animals, counting them and moving them from field to field so that they had fresh grass always. If they fell in a dyke they would use a block and tackle and soon have them pulled out. When the marshes were dry, water would be let into the dykes from the river. 'Yoiton', to test the river water, used to dip

26

Berney Arms : Past and Present.

the end of his walking stick into the river and taste the wet end of the stick. Only if it was not salty would he let the water into the dykes. In the summertime the thistles would be topped and 'Yoiton' would employ local men to help. Local men would also help with cattle droving when the cattle were ready to leave the marshes. They would take them to Wickhampton where they would be picked up by cattle trucks to be taken to market.

Cutting the hay was done the old fashioned way with either a tractor or 'Kitty' the horse pulling a grasscutter. After it had lain for a few days a 'turner' or 'kicker' would be used to turn the hay over and when it was ripe a dragrake was used to rake the hay up and it was put in haycocks till it was time to fetch it in by tractor or horse and cart. The men would be working until dark doing this.

Reed cutting was another way of earning a shilling or two. 'Yoiton' rented reedbeds at Fritton and Belton and employed people to do the work. The reeds would be cut and dried and bunched and a wherry would take them to Reedham.

'Yoiton' was paid for maintaining the gateways by filling in the ruts and mending the gates when needed. He was also paid to maintain a motorboat in case it was needed for emergencies and medical reasons.

When 'Yoiton' first moved to Ashtree farm he would take his milk to Reedham by boat. Often he would pick up his nephew, Ivan Mace, at Seven Mile and take him to Reedham so he could go to school. In later years the churns of milk would be taken by horse and cart to Berney Arms station and put on the train to Reedham.

The Acle sale on a Thursday was a meeting place for the marshmen, and workers, if they could get the day off. They would do their selling and buying and as there were two pubs nearby they would have a good old yarn while quenching their thirst. 'Yoiton' liked his drink. Visitors to Ashtree farm were always welcomed with a rum or hot-toddy. 'Yoiton' would always be wearing a collar and tie and his cap, and until a few years before he retired he wore buskins.

A story is told of 'Yoiton' that he took his horse to be shod at Reedham, left the horse at the blacksmiths and went to meet his mates at the pub. When he went back to collect his horse, a little worse for drink, he sat on it the wrong way round, much the ammusment of everyone there. Another tale is that on another occasion he returned home without his horse after he had been for a drink.

Another tale about 'Yoiton' is that when the River Board were working at Berney one time, he got them to use one of their boats to ferry a bull across from Berney to the Island for him. With 'Yoiton' holding the halter the bull was quite happy with the trip. This was 'Yoiton's way of saving money by not having to pay for a round trip by lorry.

'Yoiton' bought a new bull at one time and after a short time at the farm it became obvious something was wrong. It would go around half crazed, and one day our father found the bull in a distressed state. It head-butted a wrought-iron wheelbarrow up through the cowshed roof. Mr Williams coaxed the bull with feed into a stall in the cowshed, and by balancing himself against the back of the wall over the feedboxes he managed to feed a rope through the ring in the bulls nose and tie it secure. The bull was sold shortly afterwards to another marsh farmer who could not handle the bull either. A week later it had been taken to the abattoir.

'Yoiton' loved to go to the races at Yarmouth, meeting up with his friends. These were his days out, unless he went to the 'Derby' or to the Norfolk Show. Holidays away were not thought about for a marshman or their workers, as the cows needed milking, and the cattle needed to be looked after every day, and they could not be left for long.

When interviewed by Fyfe Robertson for the 'Tonight' programme in 1960 'Yoiton' said "I would not move if you paid me twenty pounds a week and free board. My father lived here, my grandfather lived here, and they both lived till they died." 'Yoiton' became something of a local celebrity, talking on the radio and appearing on television, while his photograph often appeared in various magazines, and several articles about him appeared in the local newspapers.

Figure 23. Left: Reggie Hewitt at the Berney Arms Mill. Photo supplied by Linda Smith. Right: Stanley and Barbara Hewitt by the Berney Mill. They were custodians of the mill for about 25 years. Photograph supplied by Stanley and Barbara Hewitt.

'Yoiton' loved to have a yarn with everyone including the holiday makers, many of whom would buy him a drink, and on one occasion Rod Clark recalls a time in the Berney Arms Inn when 'Yoiton' in conversation with a female holidaymaker said "I must go now and move my bullocks". The lady said, "Bullocks! Don't you mean cows?". "No", said 'Yoiton', "I mean bullocks". The lady then asked "So what is the difference between a bullock and a cow?". 'Yoiton' replied with a smile, " Bollocks", and departed.

During 'Yoiton's last few years at Berney Arms he became the local Berney postman and custodian of the old Berney Mill. In the autumn of 1962 he and his wife moved from Ashtree Farm to Cobholm, Great Yarmouth, but 'Yoiton' for another two years continued to travel from Cobholm to the Breydon Pump which he still operated. Shortly after he moved, aged 71, he also got himself a job for a short time at the Merchant House at Yarmouth where he could meet people and have a yarn.

After Annie Marie died in December 1973 he moved back to Ashtree Farm to live with his son. When he took ill they had to get a motorboat to take him from Berney to Burgh Castle to an ambulance waiting there to take him to hospital, because an ambulance could not get across the rutted marsh tracks safely. He died in hospital in June 1974, at the age of 82. Sadly an error was made somehow and his headstone in Burgh Castle churchyard gave his age as 84.

BERNEY ARMS MILL.(TG465049)

Berney Arms High Mill is a tarred brick tower mill. No definite date is known, though it is thought to have been built about 1865 by Edward Stolworthy of Great Yarmouth. It is seven floors and stands 70 feet high with an external diameter of 28 feet at ground level and has a

Figure 24. The author in front of Berney Arms High Mill in 1999.

boat shaped cap.

Originally, according to Harry Apling in 'Norfolk Corn Windmills', it had four double shuttered sails, outer pair 10 bays of 3, inner pair 7 bays of 3 with 2 innermost bays of 4, but when restored each sail had only 2 bays of 3 vanes in the 3rd and 4th bays from the tip. It has an 8-bladed fantail, an iron gallery, a chain pole and an iron stage on the third floor. The scoop wheel which was used for draining the marshes is 24 feet in diameter and stands separate from the mill.

Berney Arms : Past and Present.

Earlier mills have been sited here. A drainage mill was shown at this location on Faden's map 1797. In 1847 a five storey mill was used for grinding cement, and in 1828 the mill here was used to drive circular saws for the sawmill. More details are given in the next section.

The present mill was originally used for crushing clinker to produce cement powder and it was part of the cement works which once stood to the east of the mill. After 1883 it was used only as a drainage mill, and would have been worked by the marshmen William Hewitt, ('The King'), Jimmy Hewitt, ('Wesmacot') and Henry Hewitt, ('Yoiton'), until 1949 when it was replaced by an electric pump.

In William's day if there was any trouble at the mill they would set the sails topsail, that is with one sail pointing straight up, so the millmen working the other mills miles away across the levels would see and the word went out. In the very old days they would signal to each other in this way if a cargo of smuggled goods was on its way up the river. It is said that smugglers often used the mills to hide their contraband.

The marshes often flooded in the winters when the winds were not strong enough to turn the windmill sails and sometimes the waterlogged marshes would freeze in the ice-cold winters, and the locals would go skating over the frozen marshes.

The Berney Arms High mill stopped at 10:15 on the morning of 3 January 1949. The new electric pump which took over had mains electricity brought to it along the river wall from the Breydon Pump. The Berney pump has one 70 horsepower electric motor and can pump up to about 50 tons of water a minute. The pump is now only rarely used as the RSPB keep the water levels high, and any surplus water is taken by the larger Breydon pump.

Some custodians of the mill since it has been open to the public have been Mr Farrant, Mr Patterson, 'Yoiton', Barbara and Stanley Hewitt, and Mrs Susan Loughlin.. The mill underwent repairs to the sails in 2007 but there is no custodian on site at the mill today.

When the mill was open to the public in the 1950's the entrance fee was one shilling (5p).

The sailing club often visited Berney Arms in the 1950's and hammocks were hung around inside the mill. As children, when 'Yoiton' was custodian, we often went and lay in the hammocks and surprised the visitors.

'Elizabeth Simpson' the converted Yarmouth lifeboat made trips from Yarmouth to Berney Mill in the summer months for several years.

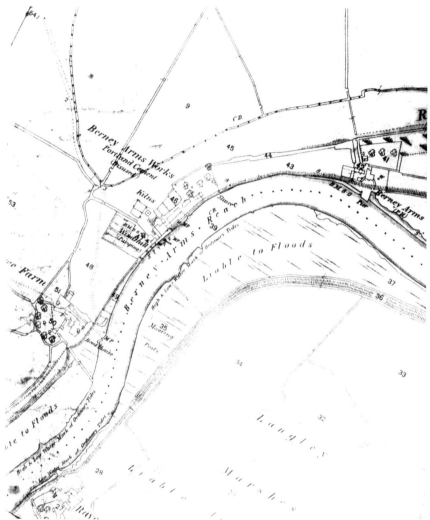

Figure25. Ordnance Survey Map 1883 showing the Cement Works.

Figure26.

The Reedham Cement Works at Berney Arms in 1874 from a painting by Charles Harmony Harrison.

Berney Arms : Past and Present.

The Berney Arms High Mill and remains of the cement works kilns around 1900.
The cottages 6 & 7 and the Bungalow are shown on the right of the picture.
Courtesy of Robert Malster.

Figure 27.

Berney Arms : Past and Present.

CEMENT WORKS.(TG465049)

A few yards beyond the mill there was once a cement works and sawmill, presumably a hive of activity many years ago. The mill, and former windmills, were in fact part of these cement works.

The cement works belonged to the Berney family and although the Berneys did not live here, Thomas Trench Berney was listed in Whites Directory of 1836 as 'Brick & Cement Maker, Sawmills'; as owner of 'Brickyard and Marsh, Factory, Mill and Yard' in the Tithe Award of 1841, and in 1868 in Harrods Directory as a 'Portland Cement Manufacturer'

The newspaper adverts below give lots of information about the cement works, windmills, sawmills and brickworks as well as mentioning the cottages, pub and a 'comfortable residence' which would be Ashtree Farmhouse.

Norfolk Chronicle, dated 10th. February 1821:-
'To be Let   For a Term of Years
A most desirable Situation for Trade at Reedham in the county of Norfolk, consisting of a Kiln, Windmill and Warehouses, with every convenience for the manufactory of Roman Cement. Also an extensive Brick Ground with an unlimited extent of brick earth and most complete drying sheds, coal and sand houses requisite for making bricks. Also a Public House called Berney Arms and with or without a quantity of marsh land adjoining.
The above premises are well situated by the side of the river distant 5 miles from Yarmouth by water and near the junction of three navigable rivers, the Yare, the Waveney and the Bure. The whole of the buildings are so arranged with an extensive quay that the manufactory can be carried on without any land carriage.
Apply to Mr Woodrow, St. George's, Norwich.'

Norfolk Chronicle, 20th April 1822 :-
'To   builders, Plasterers   & Bricklayers, The   Improved Roman Or Parkers Cement Manufactured   By Steam maybe had in any quantity of the best quality and on the most   reasonable terms   at   the REEDHAM CEMENT   WORKS near   Great Yarmouth, Norfolk. The   cement   is unequalled   for

Figure 28. The Berney Mill and cement works circa 1890.
Courtesy of Stuart Press.

34

Berney Arms : Past and Present.

stuccoing old or new buildings, for building Docks, Wharfs, Bridges, Malting Cisterns, for laying terraces and all kinds of floors, being much cheaper than stone or pavement and superior where wet or frost are to be resisted. Windowsills, coping, chimney potts, cornerstones, pump troughs and sinks made to order. N.B. best wall burnt clamp bricks may also be had of the best quality and in any quantity.
All orders addressed to Thos. Kenworthy, Dukes Head, Quay, Yarmouth or to Messrs. Squire & Edwards, Dukes place Norwich will be strictly attended to.'

Note: Roman and Parkers cement are hydraulic cements which harden under water and contain lime. Parkers cement is named after Joseph Parker who was a cement pioneer in the eighteenth century.

Norfolk Chronicle, 2 April 1825:-
'REEDHAM SAW MILLS & CEMENT WORKS
Foreign Timber, Deals, Battens, Spars, Pantiles, Splines and Coopers' Stuff are cut to order on the shortest notice and on the most reasonable terms at these works, where may be had Herring Barrel Staves and Heading, Brush backs and Boards and any article in the Sawing line executed in the neatest manner'.

Norfolk Chronicle, 13 September 1828:-
'REEDHAM CEMENT WORKS
Sawing Mills, Brick & Tile Kilns.
To be Let For a Term of Years, with Immediate Possession,
At Reedham in the County of Norfolk.
A Well Established CONCERN situate at the junction of two Navigable Rivers, near the Sea Port Town of Great Yarmouth, consisting of a Kiln, manufactory, ten horse steam engine, extensive warehouses,

Figure 29. View of the foundations of the Cement Works taken from the mill in 1973. An outline of the footings of cottages 6&7 are just visible at the top of the photograph and the Bungalow footings are also visible just below this. Photograph supplied by Peter Allard.

counting room, quay, roomy yard and two cottages for workmen. Also a very powerful Windmill with patent sails, driving seven circular saws and a deal frame particularly adapted for Sawing for Herring Barrels, in which a very considerable trade is now carried on. The Windmill is capable of being converted to any other Trade requiring

35

great power, as it is built to draw four pairs of Stones. Also a capital Tile Kiln with extensive and well arranged tile sheds, two Brick Kilns with spacious grounds adjoining, coal bins and other requisite buildings, four good cottages for workmen; an unlimited supply of fine Brick and Tile earths upon the premises.
A Comfortable Residence with or without 150 Acres of fine Grazing Land may be hired with the above.Apply to Messrs. Woodrow & Newton, Norwich. (Letters to be post paid). Principals only will be treated with.'

Norfolk Chronicle, 25 June 1836:-
'THE REEDHAM CEMENT WORKS & SAWMILLS
Near Great Yarmouth.
To be Let and Entered upon Immediately
They consist of a Ten horse Steam Engine and powerful Patent Sail Windmill (capable of driving three pair of Corn Stones). The Engine and Mill are employed in Grinding Cement, Sawing and Draining Marshes for which a rent is paid. They are well adapted for Bone, Oil or Corn Mills and being on the confluence of three large rivers running into Norfolk and Suffolk command an extensive trade.
There is also a brick and tile Ground and Kilns to be Let with or without the above.
Apply to Mr. J. Brown, Morton Hall or on Saturdays at the Norwich Corn Market.'

Norfolk Chronicle, 6 March 1847:-
'THE REEDHAM CEMENT WORKS
Saw & Water Mills Driven by Steam and Wind Power near Great Yarmouth.
To be Let and Entered upon Immediately
They consist of a 12 horse Steam Engine, a five storey Brick Tower Patent sail Windmill, able to drive four pair of Stones with Corn gear complete and now employed by Messrs. Ramsden and Co. In the Cement Trade; situate at the mouth of the Norwich River and commanding the Main Rivers of Norfolk and Suffolk, with extensive Quays and depth of water for Seaborne Vessels. The station on the Railroad from Yarmouth to Norwich and London and the North is within five minutes walk and a tram road can be laid to the same, being on the dead level. The situation and Works are well calculated for Bone, Oil or Malt Trade.
To be Sold
A powerful 6 horse BONE MILL by Scales and Hutchinson of Newcastle.'
Note: Although a station and railway line existed by 1847 there never has been any sidings constructed at Berney for loading and unloading goods vehicles.

Norfolk Chronicle, 3 March 1860:-
'THE REEDHAM CEMENT WORKS driven by Steam and wind power near Yarmouth.
TO BE LET for a term of years.
They consist of a 12-horse steam-engine and a 24-horse brick tower patent sail wind mill late in the occupation of Mr. Reynolds, in the cement trade, situate at the mouths of the Norwich and Beccles rivers with water communications to most parts of Norfolk and Suffolk. The Berney Arms Station on the railway from Yarmouth to Norwich, London and the north is within five minutes walk and a tram road to the same may be laid at small expense. The situation is well calculated for the manufacture of Portland cement, being in the immediate neighbourhood of an inexhaustible supply of the best materials for making the same.
Apply to Mr. Nesbitt, Morton near Norwich.'

Berney Arms : Past and Present.

Figure 30. Berney locals outside the Bungalow circa 1920. From the left : 'Yoiton', his aunt Rose Emma Hewitt, standing on the fence his youngest brother Ernest Hewitt, youngest sister Ada Hewitt, older brother Bob Hewitt, Billy Farrow and Gertie Farrow (nee Bruce, the daughter of Rose Emma Hewitt). The bay windows of the parlour are shown behind them.

Note: Portland cement is an hydraulic cement developed and patented by Joseph Aspin in 1824. It's predictable properties are the result of precise proportioning of it's constituents.

The cement was manufactured from a mixture of chalk and clay which would be baked in the kilns to form a clinker. This was then ground into a powder. The chalk was delivered from Norwich or Whitlingham by wherry and the mud was either dredged from Breydon Water or brought from Oulton Broad by wherry.

An examination of the census records, listed later, shows that some of the Berney residents worked at the cement works. In 1851 there is no one listed as a worker at the cement works but in 1861 there are four residents working here as cement labourers. In 1871 only one person is listed as a cement worker but eleven men are entered as labourers. Of these some would be working for the railway, some would be agricultural labourers, but some would probably be labouring at the cement works. In the 1881 census one person is listed as a cement worker and two people are Watermen, at least one of these, George Thaxter, worked for the cement company transporting cement and clinker between the Berney and Burgh Castle Works by wherry. He is mentioned in 'Black Sailed Traders' as the skipper of the wherry 'Herbert' which was owned by the Burgh Castle Company.

The Burgh Castle Cement Company occupied the Berney works from the early 1870's. The Berney works were eventually closed down about 1880 but the mill continued to grind clinker which was transported by wherry to Burgh Castle until 1883, after which time the mill was used as a drainage mill.

The remains of four old wherries have lain for many years near the new Breydon electric pumphouse and Stone corner on Breydon. All four wherries were scuttled here to protect this exposed part of the estuary wall. It is firmly believed that these vessels were once owned by Burgh Castle Cement and Brick Company. In 1892 four of the older wherries out of a fleet of six, were retired to Breydon north wall. The fleet of six comprised the 'Britannia', 'Fanny',

Berney Arms : Past and Present.

'Frank', 'Herbert', 'Mary' and 'Morton'.

Some of the Berney Arms cement works buildings stood for several years after closure of the factory, and Ernest Hewitt recalls that his father Thomas Edward Hewitt used one of the old cement works kilns as his blacksmith shop into the 1920's.

The last remains of the cement kilns were bulldozed down about 1950 and the rubble was used to fill the old dyke leading to the mill which was no longer required after a new dyke had been cut to the new electric pump. A few bits of the foundations and rubble remained visible when I lived at Berney but they have since been removed.

BUNGALOW.

A few yards past the cement works stood the bungalow, it was built of grey bricks with a slate roof. The bungalow was originally built and used as an office for the cement works.

On the 1891 census Isaac Hewitt, was living here and worked as a millwright. His wife Emma Hewitt used the parlour as a nursery school for a few years around 1900.

Some Occupants of the Bungalow

Name	Notes
Isaac & Rose Emma Hewitt & family	1891 - parlour used as nursery school
Reggie &Blanche Mace & family	1930's till 1945
Aubrey & Dennis Appleton	bought it from Berney Estate in mid 1940's
Mr Hitchcock & family	1950's early 1960's
Mr Baker	circa 1963 - made a spring & capped it
Mr Bob Manning	bought & demolished the bungalow circa 1969

Ivan Mace whose family lived here recalls it had a large room facing the river and sectioned off to make two rooms, a bedroom facing the station, a big parlour facing the mill, a kitchen facing the mill and a living room facing the station. A wooden toilet was down the garden under an oak tree. The bungalow was bought by Bob Manning in 1969 and demolished the same year.

Figure 31. View of the bungalow and cottages 6/7 in the 1950s. (D Pyett)

Figure 32. Large coaster boat passing Berney Arms in 1959. Photograph from Edward Roberts.

Figure 33. Golden galleon in 1955 when she made river trips from Gt. Yarmouth to Reedham.

Berney Arms : Past and Present.

COTTAGES 6&7. (TG465051)

A few yards past the Bungalow, stood the semi-detached cottages 6&7, built with red bricks and tile roofs. These, I believe, were built originally for the cement workers.

Violet Mace recalls that Stanley High lived at no. 7 in the 1920's, and some other occupants at 6 and 7 were Blanche Hewitt, Elsie Bailey, and during the war years Billy Farrow and his wife Gertie. During the war years evacuees from Yarmouth would spend the nights at Berney Arms to get away from the bombing, and Mrs Richardson and her parents, the Dentons, lodged at no.7 with the Farrows. After the war Allen and Ruth Brackenbury lodged at no. 7, with the Farrows having no.6. The last occupants before we moved in were the Hunt family. Ralph Hunt worked for the River Board.

Each cottage had two bedrooms upstairs, a living room and kitchen downstairs. With only two bedrooms one wonders how, looking at the 1891 census, a family of two adults and six children managed in number 7. Quite a houseful!

They probably relied on rainwater from the roof going into guttering and down into a brick-lined cistern at the rear and water tanks at the front, the same as we did when we lived there from 1959 to 1963. There was no well or spring at the property.

When we moved there from number 1 cottage in 1959, after Vera and Ralph Hunt and their two children moved to the station cottages, these two cottages had already been converted into one dwelling with a door in between the two front living rooms and another door connecting the two front bedrooms. The cottages had been connected on the top floor many years earlier according to Bob Mace who lived there when he was fourteen years old, but he does not remember a connection on the ground floor at that time. Consequently we had two back doors facing the railway station , two front doors facing the river, and two staircases one each end of the building, though the stairs in the no.6 side was unsafe and not used

The back room (no. 6 side) had an old fashioned fire grate, and a big old table upon which stood a bucket of rainwater with a jug at its side ready for use. In the winter months the water in the bucket would freeze and we would have to break the ice with the jug. In the front room there was a coal fire cooking stove. The front room on no.7 side had a fireplace and the back room had a 'copper' with a fire beneath for boiling water on a washday. This was usually a Monday. As we had no running water the copper would be filled by hand with rainwater from the water tank and then emptied by hand using a handcup scoop. When the tank was low we would get a churn of water from nearby Ashtree farm which had its own spring. The water from the spring was a brownish colour as it was full of 'iron'.

The toilet was outside, it was a little wooden hut. Inside was a wooden bench with a hole in it and a bucket underneath. Easterly winds got very bad one winter night and the toilet was blown over when brother Derek was inside.

We never had electricity and we used candles, mantle lamps and Tilley lamps.

41

Berney Arms : Past and Present.

Charlie Waters, of Bessey & Palmer, delivered our coal once a year during the summer months because the tracks across the marshes were impossible to get through in the winter.

The little window in our bedroom facing the farmhouse was badly fitted and we had a piece of cardboard from the grocery box to stop the draught. Sometimes it would go missing if mother had run out of paper and cardboard to light the copper or the fire. The draft would remain till the next grocery box was delivered.

Breakfast was bacon, eggs, mushrooms and all the trimmings fried in a pan placed on sticks burning in the fire of the backroom of no.6 side. Any black bits of charcoal you just pulled them out!

**Figure 34. The Wherry Albion being refloated near cottages 6 & 7
in January 1960. Photograph courtesy of Eastern Daily Press.
From 1953 she was chartered and carried scouts and other
passengers, and in 1961 she stopped carrying 'dirty' cargo.**

On January 1st. 1960 the wherry 'Albion' sank outside these cottages. The wherry 'Illtry' sank the same day around the bend. The Albion was pulled

Berney Arms : Past and Present.

up on the 6 and 7th January. My sister and I were offered 6d by a photographer from the Yarmouth Mercury to have our picture taken sat on the mast which lay on the river bank.

Figure 34 shows the 'Albion' as she is being pulled up.

Large ships, such as Polly-M, Jim-M and Ellen-M, etc. made regular trips from Yarmouth to Cantley and Norwich and back with their cargos of coal, oil, wood, beet etc. and some would occasionally collide into the pilings of the riverbank. I remember one time it was late at night and everyone was in bed when all of a sudden there was a huge bang. The houses shook and everywhere was lit up. A ship had gone into the pilings near the side of our house. It was believed that the skipper was a bit 'tipsy'. Whenever a boat collided into the bank, my brother, sister, and myself would go to granddad, 'Yoiton', and ask him to ring up the Port and Haven Commission authorities to report the collision. We would have to draw a sketch to show where it had happened and for this we three children got £1 each, which was a lot of money in the late 1950's and early 1960's.

Many other boats and ships went past Berney Arms, including port tugs towing lighters, and we often sat writing down their names and numbers.

Pleasure boats regularly came down the Yare past Berney Arms and one of these was the Golden Galleon which started river trips in 1950 from Yarmouth to near Reedham and back. Built of wood this boat was a motor launch (ML162) during WW11. When the boat went passed our house the captain always called out a 'hello' to us children and when it was one of our birthdays he would get the passengers to sing 'Happy Birthday'. We were once given a free trip on the Golden Galleon and went with our mother and nanny, Annie Hewitt. We walked across the marshes to get the train, as normal, to go to Yarmouth, and walked to the Quay to board the boat to enjoy the trip across Breydon and down the river past our house.

The Golden Galleon usually did three trips a day, morning, afternoon, and early evening, and at weekends she did a late evening disco trip.

In 1952 the Eastern Princess and Golden Galleon used to make trips down the river Yare together . They were all lit up and made quite a spectacle and a lot of noise.

Figure 35. The JIM-M photographed from the Langley Detached Mill in September 1948. Ashtree farmhouse is just visible behind the ship. The new electric pumphouse and the Berney mill as well as the Bungalow and 6/7 cottages are also just visible. Supplied by Rod Clark.

Berney Arms : Past and Present.

The Resolute made trips down the Waveny and on its return trip it would be stoking up as it passed Burgh Castle and it seemed as though it would be racing the Golden Galleon across Breydon.

The Golden Galleon was painted in its original battleship grey once again and was moored up at Reedham not far from the swing bridge and opposite Pearsons boatyard, but it has since been scraped.

Every Sunday yachts could be seen racing from Burgh Castle to Berney and back.

In the summer of 1960 Fyfe Robertson and a team from the BBC came to Berney Arms to make a short film for the Tonight programme presented by Cliff Michelmore. He interviewed my grandad Henry Hewitt and dad Joseph Williams. The film was shown on 2nd. September 1960. We did not have electricity in 6/7 cottage so we watched it at Ashtree farm with nanny and grandad. After the film was broadcast we were sent jigsaws, comics and paints etc. by the people who had watched the programme.

Figure 36. Jack Hunt, river inspector, talking to his brother Ralph and Ralph's son Kavan near the style by 6 and 7 cottages, circa 1953. Photograph supplied by Kavan Hunt.

Father, Joseph Williams grew vegetables: onions, carrots, radishes, lettuce and rhubarb in the garden. We had a table near the river wall and sold the vegetables to the holiday makers, they were allowed to cut their own lettuces. Lettuces were also taken to Yarmouth market to be sold. Sweet Williams were also grown and sent to Newcastle. There should be twelve bunches to a box but the flowers were so big we could only get eleven to a box without crushing them.

At one time dad had four calves, and had a shed for them at the bottom of the garden. They all had names: Spot, Sparkler, Toby and Tip. We had eleven cats, a one-legged goose called Hoppey and a dog called Moss. At one time, when a noise was heard in the roof, dad put one of the cats in the roofspace thinking the noise may be from mice or rats. That cat was never seen again!

44

Berney Arms : Past and Present.

All three of us children went to school in Yarmouth by train, and at one time there was a rail strike so we went by boat to Burgh Castle and a taxi picked us up there and took us to Yarmouth. We had one cat that would walk over the marshes to come and meet us when we got off the train.

I started work in Yarmouth in September 1961, aged 15. I was up at 6 o'clock in the mornings to get ready to walk over the marshes to catch the train at 7:30. With my first weeks wages I bought an electric hair dryer. This became a joke as we had no electricity and it was not used until we moved to Cobholm, Great Yarmouth.

**Figure 37. Cottages 6&7 in the 1950s.
Photograph from David Pyett.**

The last winter we lived at Berney Arms 1962/3 was a bad winter. I remember leaving home at seven each morning to go to work and catching the five thirty from Gt. Yarmouth getting me home around six o'clock. Easterly winds blew so cold over the marshes giving chapped legs and chilblains and a determination that any coypu rats around can forget me. With the light from the Berney Pump shining it felt as though I had company as I walked from the station through the mud, and who knows what else, towards that light at the pump. I knew that when I got to the big arch gate I was nearly home, and once inside there would be a lovely roaring fire and I could thaw out, have a nice meal and do it all again the next day.

We moved from Berney Arms in July 1963 and 'Chinky' Carter moved our furniture and belongings on his truck. These cottages were pulled down shortly after we moved out in 1963, and the bricks and rubble were used to build up the river wall.

COYPUS

When we lived at Berney the coypu was in abundance on the marshes. They would gather around the liggers at the dykes and on a pitch black night they would be very frightening as they moaned. We often had to make the choice between walking on the ligger with three or four coypus on it or walking through the deep mud at the marsh gates. The mud won every time.

Fully grown coypus were about three feet long and looked like very large humpbacked rats. Their origins were in South America and they were imported for fur farms but escaped captivity and colonised the marshlands in the 1930's. The fur was known as 'Nutria'. We were always told that someone in Burgh Castle had kept them and they had escaped. Also there was a tale that they had come from Brundel.

Although they were herbivorous and ate the grasses, reeds and rushes they could be nasty when they were approached and I found them quite scary.

Berney Arms : Past and Present.

The Barnes family at the pub had a dog called 'Rusty' and it was always chasing the coypus. It was fortunate not to get injured. On one occasion I know of, Alan Brackenbury's dog was dragged into the dyke by an injured coypu which had grabbed the dog by the throat and the dog was almost drowned. Alan himself was also badly bitten on the wrist by a coypu. He had shot one and it then fell into a dyke. He put his hand into the dyke to retrieve the animal only to be bitten on the wrist. Alan Brackenbury used to send the coypu pelts he had to a furrier in London and he would get as much as fifteen shillings for a good skin. The coypus were crafty creatures, I remember father approaching one that he thought was dead when it snapped at him and he hit it with the butt of his twelve bore. Before the coypu rat was dead he had broken the stock of his gun.

Figure 38 . Some Hewitt family members outside the old inn, circa 1911.
Back: Harriet Hewitt and 'Yoiton', left Blanche, sitting Eliza holding
Ernest and Bob holding Ada. Photograph supplied by Mr Sid Gibbs.

The marshmen told tales of huge coypu and a prize of £6 was offered for anyone who could catch one weighing 22 pounds or more. 'Yoiton' took one over to the Stracey Arms public house to claim the reward, and on the scales it weighed 22 pounds exactley. When it was lifted by the tale, however, a huge stone fell out of its mouth, and 'Yoiton' was given a pint of beer for his cheek.

During the 1950's the number of coypu had risen so high that the authorities in attempting to control their numbers paid the marshmen to kill them. According to Stanley Hewitt, on the island at Langley marshes gun cartridges were provided free, while at Berney Arms they were paid 2s per tail. Later they were paid 2s 6d per tail at Berney and 2 shillings at Langley marshes. Stanley Hewitt remembers one time when he was at Berney he posted a package of tails on Christmas Eve. A few days later the post office contacted him to say they could not deliver the package because the offices were closed, and that the package smelled awful!

I have heard a tale that Coypus have been used as meat to fill meat pies, and that some marsh folk fried or casseroled the meat, adding herbs and spices. It was supposed to taste like rabbit or hare. At one time a man from Cambridge came to Berney to look at the coypus with the idea of canning their meat for sale to the public. This idea never took off. There was one local Berney family who cooked coypus in a copper at the bottom of their garden and if you were walking nearby it smelled good. At the other extreme in other villages some people kept baby coypus as pets and walked them around on a lead.

In spite of the numbers shot the coypu continued to increase in population; they could have two litters per year each litter of about six to eight babies. In the early 1960's an attempt was made to exterminate the coypu and squads of men were employed to go about setting traps and shooting the coypus. These men were often to be encountered after dark going about their business of controlling the pests, and bumping into a gang of strangers in the pitch dark on the marshes was itself very scary. The extermination of the coypu was aided by the harsh winter of 1962/3 which probably did more to wipe them out than all of the other control measures employed.

BERNEY ARMS INN. (TG468052)

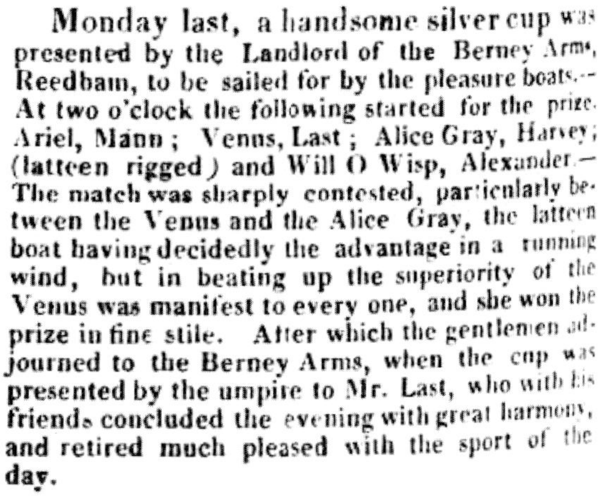

Monday last, a handsome silver cup was presented by the Landlord of the Berney Arms, Reedham, to be sailed for by the pleasure boats. At two o'clock the following started for the prize. Ariel, Mann ; Venus, Last ; Alice Gray, Harvey; (latteen rigged) and Will O Wisp, Alexander. — The match was sharply contested, particularly between the Venus and the Alice Gray, the latter boat having decidedly the advantage in a running wind, but in beating up the superiority of the Venus was manifest to every one, and she won the prize in fine stile. After which the gentlemen adjourned to the Berney Arms, when the cup was presented by the umpire to Mr. Last, who with his friends concluded the evening with great harmony, and retired much pleased with the sport of the day.

Figure 39. Newspaper cutting fromSeptember 1831.

The Berney Arms Inn stands approximately 250 yards from where 6/7 Cottages once stood. The Berney Arms was probably built in the eighteenth century although it does not appear on Faden's map of 1797. It is situated by the side of the river Yare close to Breydon Water where the Waveney River meets the Yare. It was used in days of old by wherrymen, the local cement and brick workers, wildfowlers, fisherman and poachers and in those days the beer was delivered by wherry. Today it is mainly used by boating holiday makers, walkers and birdwatchers and is only open from mid-March to the end of October.

Berney Arms : Past and Present.

In 1821 the Inn, along with the cement works, brickworks and marshes, was 'To Let' according to an advert appearing in Norfolk Chronicle dated 10th. February, and reproduced in an earlier section on the cement works. The inn was, like the other buildings in Berney, owned by the Berney family.

In 1833 Primitive Methodist missionaries came from Great Yarmouth looking for followers and at this time the 'chapel' they used for their meetings was the publicans parlour. Arthur H. Patterson in 'Hayloft to Temple', in 1903, recorded that there were seven Berney Arms members of the church in 1849, but that in 1879 and 1902 there were no members. In his book 'The Cruise of the Walrus' he tells of one Sunday when he, as a youth in the 1870's, went with the regular preacher John Britton and laypreacher George Mayman to the Inn, being rowed across by two Berneyites from Burgh Castle to a service that was attended by only two locals.

Roy Clark in 'Black Sailed Traders' recounted a tale of a grim occurance:-

'...during the Burgh Castle Water Frolic in 1863, when two men slipped off the hatches of the wherry 'Rigby' and had their heads almost severed from their bodies. They were laid out in a shed adjoining the Berney Arms Inn...'

After the pub lost its licence in 1909, according to Ernest Hewitt, it was used as a farmhouse by his parents. Several other families later occupied and lived in the building but it was rapidly getting in a bad state and in the 1940's the roof and some of the upper walls were in need of repair. Some of the land by the pub was sold in 1941 to Mr. William James Lacey. The building was left vacant for a few years until the derelict old inn was bought from the Berney family by the brothers Aubrey and Dennis Appleton for £40 in about 1947. According to Ron Carter, the brothers pulled up the floor boards to repair their boat, and according to Bob Mace, they took down the doors for firewood, making the place even worse. The brothers at that time were living in the Bungalow. When Reg Mathews bought the old inn for £250 he

BERNEY ARMS, REEDHAM.

FAST-SAILING CUTTER BOAT IN FIRST-CLASS CONDITION, TWO GUN PUNTS, FOUR SUITS OF SAILS, NEW BALLOON JIB, LEAD AND IRON KEELS AND BALLAST, SHEET-LEAD AND COPPER, MASTS, NEW SPARS, BOAT'S STORES AND RIGGING IN VARIETY, LOADED SWIVEL-GUN, CARTRIDGES, WORK BENCHES, VICES, LONG SACK ROPE AND GEARING, HEAVY IRON SPINDLES, STONE NUTS, LARGE SPUR AND OTHER HEAVY IRON WHEELS, CEMENT STONES; ALSO A FEW LOTS OF USEFUL HOUSEHOLD FURNITURE AND OTHER EFFECTS.

THE SALE TO COMMENCE AT THREE O'CLOCK IN THE AFTERNOON; ARRANGEMENTS HAVE BEEN MADE WITH THE GREAT EASTERN COMPANY TO STOP THE AFTER-NOON TRAINS AT BERNEY ARMS. SEE CATALOGUES FOR DETAILED INFORMATION.

FRAS. CLOWES is favored with directions from G. D. Berney, Esq., to Sell by Auction, without reserve, the above, with other Effects, late the pro-perty of T. T. Berney, Esq., deceased, on Friday next, June 10th, 1870, commencing at Three o'clock in the Afternoon.

Catalogues may be obtained at the Auctioneer's Offices, Bank Chambers, Norwich, or will be posted on application.

Figure 40. Newspaper cutting from 1870.

started to repair the building. The repairs were started in 1950.

The building materials, sand, cement and shingle, for the repairs to this old wherryman's pub were carried from Norwich by the Wherry 'Albion'. The Norfolk Wherry Trust had renovated the old wherry in 1949 and in January 1950 it carried the first freight to be taken out of Norwich by sailing wherry for more than twenty seven years. There was no other way of getting these materials to such an isolated spot other than by river, since there was no railway sidings or proper roads. The pub is built of brick and blocks and has a tiled roof.

GT. YARMOUTH (near). OLD INN FARM, Berney Arms, on Broads; licensed; few vacancies July 3 tc 24, also June and September; £5 full board. Brochure.

Figure 41. Newspaper cutting from May 1954.

Mr Mathews sold the pub to Mr Forster for about £800 in about 1952, and in 1953 the old inn became a club known as 'The Old Inn (Rivercraftsmen's) Club', and was only allowed to sell bottle beers to members. Bob Mace recalls that a bottle of brown ale was 9d., but when Schofield took over a special meeting was held and the price of a bottle was put up to 10d. Mr Schofield bought the place for about £2500. He opened the pub as a guest house in the summer and took in holiday makers, offered baths to the boating holiday makers and started to charge for mooring boats.

When occupied by the Schofield family they managed to get a public-house licence back in February 1955 as the newspaper report here shows:

E.D.P. 11 February 1955:-

'New Licence for Berney Arms Inn: Was Wherrymen's Public-House

After 50 years the Old Inn, Berney Arms, the former wherrymen's public-house is to be licenced to sell liquor again. At Blofield and Walsham Brewster Sessions on Monday the Bench granted a licence subject to confirmation to Mr. Charles Leslie Schofield to sell beer, wine and spirits off the premises.

In his application Mr. Schofield said that the premises which were known as the Berney Arms had an on licence until 1902 and in those days the wherrymen used to call in for drinks. Now he wanted to cater for the people on pleasure craft, the modern counterpart of the wherries. He already provided many facilities for pleasure craft.

Mr Laurence Vine (Messrs. Humphrey Lynde & Vine), who appeared for Mr Schofield,

THE OLD INN
(RIVERCRAFTMEN'S)
CLUB

BERNEY ARMS
NORFOLK
Near GREAT YARMOUTH

Figure 42. Cover of membership card for the club. Supplied by Ron Carter.

Berney Arms : Past and Present.

said there was no access by road. The nearest licenced premises were at Reedham and Yarmouth each five miles by river.
The application was supported by Mr. Alfred George Ward of Thorpe Old Hall, chairman of Norfolk and Suffolk Broads Yachtowners Association and by Mr. P. H. Liversidge, Commodore of Yarmouth and Gorleston Sailing Club who both said that they thought that the sale of liquor at the Old Inn would improve the facilities of that part of the river for people on pleasure craft.
Henry Hewitt, farmer and marshman, at Ash Tree Farm, said he had seen men employed by him on the marshes drink water out of a dyke because they were so thirsty.'

One of the adjoining buildings was made into a shop in the late 1950's.

The Schofields sold the Berney Inn to Mr and Mrs Barnes in 1960. Mr Barnes was the first person I can remember with a motor car on the Berney Marshes. Everything was usually moved by a horse and cart, tractor and trailer, or lorry as there were, and are still are, no proper public roads. The Barnes family worked hard at the inn making a name for themselves with their home-cooked meals for the holiday makers from the yachts and cruisers as well as bird-watchers and walkers. The extension on the west side was a restaurant. When we lived at 6-7 cottages, close by, my mother Ellen Marie Williams would go along to help out and my father Joseph Williams would pluck and dress ducks for their kitchen and do odd-jobs such as grass-cutting. Mr Barnes had some holiday cruisers for hire and my sister

Figure 43. The shop and pub in 2000

Maureen and myself would go along on a Saturday morning to clean out the four fibre-glass cruisers for 2/6d which was good money at the time. These were some of the first broads cruisers to be made of fibre-glass and Barnes had showers installed in them. My father recalls the day the showers were finally installed. They were having problems and he remembers Mr Barnes looking though the paper and then telephoning someone. After he put down the phone Mr Barnes asked him if he fancied a ride out to Wroxham to look at the Boatyard he had just bought over the phone. The Barnes' business progressed and their boating business was moved to Wroxham and later became Barnes Brinkcraft which is still there today, although under different ownership. Mr Barnes wanted to build a proper roadway across the marshes from Wickhampton but the cost was too much to take on by himself and it never materialised.

Berney Arms : Past and Present.

The pub was granted a full licence in 1960 as the following newspaper report shows:

E.D.P. 1960
'FIRST FULL LICENCE SINCE 1902 TRAGEDY ON BROADS

THE OLD INN, Berney Arms, the isolated former wherry men's inn on the edge of Breydon Water, was granted a full licence by Blofield licensing justices yesterday. Supt. G. W. Bartram said he understood from the owner that the inn last had a full licence in 1902, but it had been withdrawn after a party from Burgh Castle had got drunk and three had been drowned on the return journey. The owner, Mr Charles Leslie Schofield, told the justices that he had run a registered club at the inn since 1954 and also had an off-licence shop on the premises. The inn, he said could be approached in good weather by a three-mile track from Wickhampton. It was half a mile from Berney Arms Halt, which left the main approach by the river. During the 1959 season 2000 boats had paid for moorings in front of the inn, said Mr. Schofield.

Club Members
In addition, 3000 boats had moored for periods of less than 15 minutes, while another 2000 had moored within reach of the inn. Mr. Schofield said that at least one-third of his club members were also members of the Yarmouth and Gorleston Sailing Club, which had its headquarters at Burgh Castle. The remainder were locals, Norwich or Yarmouth residents and a "hard core" of regular visitors to the Broads. The application was opposed by Charles James Farrant, of 18, Wellington Road, Yarmouth, who said he had looked after the Berney Arms Mill for the Ministry of Works for the last four and a half years. His view was that if a full licence was granted more vessels would moor at the inn. It was already a dangerous place to moor and the increased traffic would increase the danger.

No Police Opposition

Figure 44. The pub and septic tank in 2000. The septic tank was made from the bricks from Tucks Mill.

Supt. Bartram, said that although the police were not opposing the application it would not be possible to supervise the house in the normal way. Mr. W. 0. Carter (Hill & Perks). for Mr Schofield, said there had been no complaint about the running of the club or the mooring facilities. The only reason for Mr. Farrant's objection was that he did not like Mr Schofield.

The application was granted subject to confirmation, on the condition that the licence should run between March 15th and October 15th and that drinks should be served in

51

Berney Arms : Past and Present.

the dining room only with meals.'

Mr Barnes bought his spirits and beers from Stewart and Patterson in Gt. Yarmouth and it was picked up from the North Quay in Yarmouth and delivered by the Wherry Albion.

In the winter of 1962/3 the weather conditions were so bad that the Barnes family temporarily moved out of Berney Inn and rented a house in Great Yarmouth.

Figure 45. The derelict Berney Arms in 1949 before renovation. (Mathews)

The Barnes family moved to Wroxham and sold the pub in 1964 to Bob Manning, who had worked as a barman for Ken Barnes. When Bob Manning was running the pub he would have one or two parties at the pub each year. Pop stars and entertainers such as Freddie and the Dreamers, Adam Faith, The Searchers, The Swinging BlueJeans and Jimmy Tarbuck, to name a few, would go there. They were normally taken from Burgh Castle by speedboat but it has been known for some to arrive by helicopter.

When the wooden railway signal box was no longer in use Bob Manning bought it and moved it to the pub. He used it as a storeroom for his stock. He also bought the old red phone box which once stood outside the station and moved that to the pub.

The inn is not connected to mains water or sewerage but has its own spring for water and a septic tank. Mr Joseph Williams remembers the time the

Berney Arms : Past and Present.

well was being sunk when the Schofield family were occupying the inn in the 1950's. The workmen had gone down about 60 feet and had not struck water

Figure46. Berney Arms Public House. Top: circa 1960. First published in East Anglia Life, January 1963. Bottom: 2000.

and were considering giving up but he told them that the well at the farm house was nearer 80 feet down and they should go down a bit further.

The inn was connected to the mains electricity supply in the 1950's and to the telephone system. Outside there was once a public telephone kiosk.

Berney Arms : Past and Present.

In November 1973 the Inn was put up for sale by auction and bought by Robert McLaughlan, in 1974.

In 2000 the pub was bought by Raymond Hollocks and since then it has had tenants leasing the pub

The decline in river traffic over recent decades has meant the business has struggled to be a thriving concern and consequently the present owner, Mr Hollocks, has wanted to convert the pub into a dwelling house, but permission has been refused by the Broads Authority and it remains at the moment as a public house.

At the time of writing, 2016, the pub is once again up for sale.

Mr Ernest Hewitt Remembers:-

The Inn lost their licence in 1909 October 11th., after three men from Burgh Castle had come to the pub by boat and were drowned when they left the pub, presumably worse for drink. The publican at that time was a Mr Andrew.

Thomas and Eliza Hewitt moved into the unlicensed Berney Arms Pub, from the Station cottages, on March 11th 1910. There was four large rooms and two box-rooms on the first floor. It was here that Ernest Hewitt, the last of their thirteen children, was born in the living room on 24th. November 1910. Ernest like other children at Berney Arms went to school at Reedham. For several years he went to school on the 6:30 morning train and returned on the 5:00 train, making it a very long day by the time he got home.

His father, Thomas Hewitt, a blacksmith by trade, worked as a railway platelayer and kept cattle, pigs and sheep and the old inn was used as a farmhouse. Thomas also had a smithy in one of the old cement works kilns.

Ernest says his father had a pair of stuffed grebes at the inn and that he put a blue stone with them. These were left at the inn when his mother left and they were still there till McLaughlan sold the pub in 2000.

A ghost wearing a brown suit was supposedly seen on numerous occasions but Ernest Hewitt never did have the pleasure as he never did see it.

Ernest recalls working for Smithdales during the building of the Breydon Pumphouse in 1933.

After his father Thomas Hewitt died, his mother Eliza moved into number two cottage.

Mr Arnold Hewitt Remembers:-

Arnold lived at Berney Arms as a child in the 1920's and recalls that when he went to school at Reedham the signalman at the Berney station was a Mr Staff.

Coal used to be delivered to Berney by river by wherry by Billy Tooley.

They were allowed to cycle along the railway line to go to Yarmouth, which they did if they went to the cinema. They were not allowed to have a red rear light on their bikes as a red light meant danger to the train drivers.

Long after he had moved away from Berney and was employed by Mr Banham in the 1960's, Banham took on the contract to get the beer delivered to the Berney Arms pub. Arnold, having warned Mr Banham that it would be difficult to get the truck across the marsh tracks, drove the first delivery but the trailer of his wagon got stuck near the Berney railway station and he could not get it moving. They left the truck till the next morning, when with the help of a bulldozer they managed to get the truck moving again, and took the beer to Reedham instead where they got May Gurney to deliver the beer by river. After this they only delivered the beer to the Acle straight new road where it would then be taken by tractor and trailer to the pub.

MR JACK CARTER REMEMBERS:-

Way back in 1946 Jack Carter and his friends and relatives started to go eel fishing at Breydon. At first they had a tent pitched on the marsh side of Breydon Water, near the 'Dickey Works' about halfway between the inn and Lockgate mill, but later obtained a house-boat. The first house-boat was bought in 1948 and called the 'Grey Lag'. A photograph is shown in figure 48. They towed it by hand from Reedham as they walked along the river bank. They intended to moor up near the 'Dicky-Works' near a bit of marsh that never flooded but Henry Hewitt, 'Yoiton', told them they could go on a Rond on the Berney side of the river not far from the Pub. The Berney family owned the rond and 'Yoiton' was in charge of Berney's land. Soon afterwards Mr Berney sold some land which included the Rond.

When Mr Matthews, who owned the pub, bought the Rond in 1950 they then had a tenancy agreement drawn up and they had to pay a guinea a year to have the house-boat on the rond. This is reproduced below.

Figure 47. Location of houseboat.

AGREEMENT made the 22nd day of September 1950 BETWEEN REGINALD ALBERT MATTHEWS of "The Inn" Berney Arms Reedham in the county of Norfolk Market Gardener (hereinafter called the Landlord which expression where the context admits includes the persons deriving title under him) of the one part and JACK WILLIAM CARTER (Coal Roundsman) and JAMES HUBERT EDWARDS (Electrical Engineer) both of Middle Hill Reedham aforesaid (hereinafter called the Tenants which expression where the context admits includes the person deriving title under them) of the other part WHEREBY IT IS AGREED as follow:-

1. THE Landlord shall let and the Tenants shall take ALL THAT piece of land situate at Berney Arms in the parish of Reedham aforesaid forming a rectangle the sides whereof each extend in length 30 feet or thereabouts as the same is surrounded by a fence and is for the purpose of identification only more particularly delineated and shown in the plan drawn hereon and thereon coloured red TOGETHER with full right and liberty (1) to lay up and keep upon the said piece of land during the tenancy one house-boat (namely) the 'Grey Lag" which is now lying on the said piece of land and (2) to pass and repass at all reasonable times over the adjoining land of the Landlord between the tow-path coloured brown on the said plan and the said piece of land. The tenancy shall be deemed to have commenced on the 24th day of June 1950 and shall be determinable by one quarter's notice to be given by either party to the other to expire on any quarter day at the yearly rent of £l. 1. 0. payable in advance on the 24th day of June in every year during the tenancy the first payment whereof shall be made on the signing hereof in respect of the period up to the 24th day of June 1951 PROVIDED that if the tenancy shall be determined by the Landlord but not otherwise on any quarter day other than the 24th day of June the Landlord

Berney Arms : Past and Present.

will repay to the Tenants a proper proportion of the current rent for that year.

2.   THE Tenants shall not erect nor allow to be erected nor bring or allow to be brought on the said piece of land any hut fencing building structure or boat of any kind other than the house-boat now lying thereon without the consent in writing of the Landlord.

3   THE Tenants shall not assign underlet or part with the possession of the said piece of land or any part thereof without the consent in writing of the Landlord.

4.   ON the determination of the tenancy the Tenants shall remove their house-boat from the said piece of land and make good any damage to the land caused thereby.

5.   IF any rent shall be in arrear for 28 days whether legally demanded or not or there shall be any breach by the Tenants of the conditions herein contained the Landlord may re-enter on the said piece of land without giving any notice to quit and expel the Tenants therefrom.

6.   THE Landlord agrees that the Tenants paying the said rent and observing the conditions herein contained shall quietly hold and enjoy the said piece of land without any lawful interruption by the Landlord (meaning himself personally) or any person rightfully claiming under him.

AS WITNESS the hands of the parties hereto the day and year first above-written.

SIGNED by the said REGINALD ALBERT MATTHEWS in the presence of:-
E.J.RICHARDSON.
The Inn Farm, Berney Arms,
Great Yarmouth; Housekeeper.

SIGNED by the said JACK WILLIAM CARTER and JAMES HUBERT EDWARDS in the presence of:-
W. CROSS,

Figure 48. The 'Greylag' in the mid-1950's. Photograph supplied by Ron Carter.
Ship Hotel,
Reedham; Manager.

56

Berney Arms : Past and Present.

The second house-boat, called 'FourWinds', they bought in 1970 at Brundall and Jimmy Pearson of Reedham helped them to get the boat to Berney Arms. The Fourwinds is shown in the photograph in figure 49 , taken in 1972, and shows Graham Long, Jack W. Carter, Tom Carter, Jack Smith and David Carter.

At first they used to row to Berney Arms from Reedham each Saturday and row back on Sunday. After a while they left the rowboats, which they made themselves, at the houseboat, and Jack would bike down early Saturday morning and get the rowboats ready. The rowboats were shackled up to prevent anyone stealing them.

Jack dug up worms from his garden on Thursdays and Fridays and put them in a bucket of earth until he took them to the boathouse on Saturday morning. About fourty worms would be threaded lengthways onto Worsted using a home-made needle, made from an old bicycle spoke. The ends of the thread were then tied together and it was wrapped into a coil around three fingers. Another thread was passed through the coil and tied tightly. A length of thread was then attached to this along with home-made weights and to a pole at the other end. The bait was then put into the water and gently bobbed or 'babbed' up and down to attract the eels. When they had a bite they quickly raised the pole and shook the eel into the bottom of the boat. They normally babbed on a flood tide and did this on the side of the boat where the water was moving away from them.

They also sometimes fished for cucumber smelts and flounders using a butt dart and when there was three of them they would sometimes use a net. Two of them would hold the ends of the net and the third would agitate the water to drive the fish into the net.

The eels were put into a bucket with saltwater overnight and skinned the next morning.

Jack remembers going to Ashtree Farm on most Saturdays around 4 or 5 o'clock and having milk straight from the cooler. In exchange he would take some eels to 'Yoiton' the next morning.

They kept a record of their weekly catch and prepared annual reports. Below is extracts from the 1958 annual report prepared by Ron Carter.

Jack finished with eel catching in 1986.

ANNUAL REPORT FOR 1958.

This according to the weather experts has been one of the wettest summers on record and, although this has had an adverse effect on travelling, we have been extremely lucky in so far as on our numerous trips this summer we have had rain on two occasions only, the first on Sunday morning July 20th when a thunderstorm occurred from about 8 o'clock, and the second a very light shower lasting about 5 minutes on the evening of August 2nd. On no evening was there enough wind to trouble us.

Figure 49. 'FourWinds' in 1972. Photograph supplied by Jack Carter.

We started off the year with a bang! I arrived on Good Friday in order to give the boat its usual pre-season airing and discovered several windows broken and the boat ransacked. Jack and I made temporary repairs and decided that the only thing left to do was to make steel shutters for the windows. Then about a fortnight before we were due to open the season proper an outbreak of 'foot and mouth' disease occurred in cattle near Berney, but we found that it was all right for us to start on May 3rd but Jack Smith who was still 'in the bullocks' decided it would be better if he missed the opening trip.

However, Bob, Jack, Grant and I arrived on the one o'clock train and Jack and Bob started slubbing, this being the main item of work on this years agenda. Bob and I had a good night's babbing although the eels were rather small and very lazy...........

In contrast to the previous weekend, the eels were biting viciously and after an hour's fishing our babs were looking the worse for wear. However, they managed to last for an hour or so and quite a good haul was made.

According to various reports after supper, Charlie's beer was definitely off colour.......

August 16th. And I arrived first to find 'Eela' stolen. Bob, the next to arrive, and I walked as far as the 'dicky works' but couldn't see her....... Next morning we cleared up early and all took the 'Queen Mary' over to Burgh and started searching. We soon found her and towed her home and securely chained her........

The weather was kind and Jack, Bob and Jack Smith duly went. Fishing started at 7 o'clock, and although biting was slow the eels were good and the season finally finished at about 10:30 on October 25th.

Bob, Jack and I bought the boats home by tractor and trailer on November 1st.

Now to turn to results. Generally eels were rather small, but the total catch for the year was 3,582 eels. This represents an increase of 147 on last year with 8 less 'man-trips'.

Individual placings for the regulars are as follows:-

Jack Carter	*670 eels caught in*	*12 trips average 55.8*	
Bob " 925	*" "*	*14 "*	*66*
Jack Smith	*539 " "*	*11 "*	*49*
Ron Carter 1,177	*" "*	*12 "*	*98.*

Jack, as a teenager, worked at the mill at Halvergate in the early 1930's, and recalls a Mr Cafferoy (?) who lived at the old inn at Berney and who rode on horseback from Berney to Acle and returned via Halvergate Mill to collect some grain. The grain was loaded into his two saddlebags. Cafferoy, Jack believes, kept animals inside the old inn.

Many years ago Jack took some cuttings from the deep red roses growing at the Berney Station and they were still growing in his garden in 2001.

'The Song of the Inn'

Ron Carter wrote the following verse for a Christmas card which the boys at the houseboat sent to 'Yoiton', in itself it represents a brief modern, if slightly inaccurate,

Berney Arms : Past and Present.

history of the pub:

The Inn was standing empty at the finish of the war.
And then two brothers bought it and repaired the roof and door.
But to mend their little motor boat they ripped up half the floor
But its soul went marching on.

Chorus:
Glory, Glory lead the way back
Glory, Glory take a big sack.
Glory, Glory make the babs Jack.
And we'll fish from Spring till Autumn once again.

Matthews looked it over, he thought and then he bought.
He opened up a club but for his goats some land he sought.
So he bought the rond around the boat, took Jack and Bert to court.
But its soul went marching on.

CHORUS

Dick Forster was the next in line, he only stayed a year.
He worked in Peterborough in the week, weekends he came down here.
But he found the Breydon winter mud was more than he could bear.
But its soul went marching on.

CHORUS

Along came Gwen and Charlie with their money grabbing spree.
Hot baths, roast ducks, old fenders, even mooring to the quay.
The gentlemen's ablutions were the only item free.
Yet its soul went marching on.

CHORUS

But now with Ken in residence, the Inn regains its charms.
With dining room, a pleasant lounge perhaps some potted palms.
I've heard its changed from 'Berney' to the 'Ever Open Arms'.
So its soul went marching on.

CHORUS

So forget about the winter with its cold and mud and wet.
Let's think about the summer and the company we've met.
And in the coming season we may catch some big uns yet.
So we'll still go marching on.

CHORUS

....

Berney Arms : Past and Present.

Some Past Occupants of the Berney Arms Public House:

Dates Listed	Name	Description / Notes	Reference
1821	Thomas Riches	Publican	Burgh Castle Register
1826 - 1830	James Barrett	Publican	Burgh Castle Register
1836	John Cater	Victualler	Whites Directory
c.1840	William George	'Occupier', but did not live here.	Reedham Tithe Apportionment
1841 & 1845	Robert Rushmer	Victualler	Census & Whites
1851	Horace Gillbert	Innkeeper	Reedham Census
1861 & 1871	James Knights	Innkeeper	Census
1864 & 1868	Charles Knights	Victualler / a brother to James and did not live on premises.	Whites Directory Harrods Directory
not given	Mr Carver	Innkeeper	'Black-Sailed Traders'
1881 & 1883	Walter Daniels	Victualler / Farmer	Census & Whites
1886-1890	Frederick Carter	Victualler	Licence register
1891	Robert Thaxter	Publican	Reedham Census
1900 - 1910	John Andrew	Victualler	Kellys Directory
1909	John Andrew	Pub lost licence. Licence set to expire on 7 June 1910.	Licence Register
1910	Thomas & Eliza Hewitt & family	He was Railway Platelayer, Blacksmith / Farmer. They used old inn as a farmhouse.	Ernest Hewitt
c.1933	Mr Cafferoy (?) & family	Kept goats inside.	Jack Carter
c.1937 to c.1942	Fred & Lilly Hewitt & family	Fred worked Breydon Pump	Ivan Mace
c.1943	Vacant	Roof needing repair.	Ivan Mace
c.1947	Aubrey Appleton & Dennis Robertson	Aubrey was a Musician. Bought the old inn from the Berney family. Removed floorboards and doors.	Ron Carter / Bob Mace
c.1949	Reginald & Elsie Matthews & family (Marguerite and June)	He renovated the buildings in 1950 and turned it into a guesthouse.	Reg Matthews / Peppy Matthews
c.1952	Dick Forster	Club Licence obtained in 1953	Ron Carter
1954 to 1960	Charles L. Schofield & wife Gwen & family	He worked in an Electrical store in Yarmouth. Pub Off Licence was renewed in Feb. 1955 and full licence in 1960.	Joseph Williams. Gt. Yarmouth Mercury
c.1960 to 1964	Ken Barnes & family	Publican	Shelia Hutchinson
1964 to 1974	Bob Manning	Publican	Bob Manning

Dates Listed	Name	Description / Notes	Reference
1974	Briefly owned by Northampton Brewery		Ivan Mace
c.1974 to 2000	Robert McLaughlan	Publican	Sheila Hutchinson
2000	Chris Sheppard & Carole Harvey & family.	Tenants. Pub owned by Tapestry Taverns.(Ray Hollocks)	Sheila Hutchinson
2009	Tracey Bold	Tenant	Sheila Hutchinson
April 2013	Chris Dando	Tenant	Sheila Hutchinson
March 2014	JoeRoyle & MandyWebb	Tenant	Sheila Hutchinson
July 2015	Tracey Schuurman	Tenant	Sheila Hutchinson

Figure 50. Yoiton' at the Breydon pump in 1964. Photograph from Peter Allard collection.

BREYDON PUMP.(TG477070)

A diesel pump was built in 1933 and was later replaced by an electric pump. Work began on the new electric pump in 1946 and the plant, consisting of two motors, was installed by Smithdale & Sons. The new pump was officially opened in October 1948 and is capable of discharging up to 138,000 tons of water in 24 hours from the Fleet into Breydon Water.

Fred Hewitt looked after the diesel pump when he lived at the old Berney Arms pub in the late 1930's and early 1940's. Reggie Mace worked the pump when he worked for Fred Hewitt. 'Yoiton' also worked the pump after he moved into Ashtree Farm at Berney Arms and he continued to work the electric pump for a couple of years after he moved to Cobholm. Stanley Hewitt then took over from 'Yoiton' and worked the pump for a couple of years until the Drainage Board put their own man in charge.

After the 1953 floods the river wall at Breydon was rebuilt. The Great Yarmouth Mercury 10th April 1953 reported that ' Work has started to heighten and strengthen the Breydon Wall.... 12 mechanical diggers for the last three weeks have been working on it'

Berney Arms : Past and Present.

LOCKGATE MILL AND MARSH HOUSE.(TG480072)

Figure51. Lockgate Mill and marsh house in 1936. (Perry)

Lockgate Mill also known as Banham's Black Mill was a medium size tower drainage mill of four storeys built in red brick and tarred black. The brickwork stands thirty five feet high. It was not marked on Faden's map of 1797 but was marked on Bryant's map of 1826 as Freethorpe Mill, as it was in Freethorpe detached parish. It also appears on Walker's map of the same year as Duffel's Mill, and on the 1835-37 ordnance survey map and later maps in 1883 and 1904 as Lockgate Mill. When it was put up for sale in 1877 it was described as 'recently erected by Smithdales of Acle' so the existing mill was probably a rebuild.

The mill is four storeys high, about 24 feet overall diameter at the base and had four windows and two doors. It carried four patent sails which turned clockwise and drove a large external scoop wheel, 19 feet in diameter with seven inch wide paddles. The scoop wheel has been described as the second largest in Norfolk, but it could only drain the 1,000 acres of Lockgate level at periods of low tide at Breydon Water. A small steam engine was installed in the early 1900's for a time.

In 1912 Bob Banham owned and operated the mill, and during the 1920's Gordon Addison, who lived at Lockgate Farm, was the marshman who operated the mill for a while. It was last worked in about 1947 by Leonard Carter who was the marshman who lived at the marsh house next to the mill from about 1931 till about 1949.

The marsh house had a tiled roof and was built of Suffolk whites

Figure 52. Lockgate Mill in 2000.

Figure 53. The remains of the marsh house at Lockgate mill 2000.

bricks, and was tarred black the same as the mill. According to Ernest Hewitt his uncle, Jimmy Banham, lived here before Lenny Carter. Lenny Carter left here in about 1949 and moved to High's marsh house on the Halvergate Fleet. Jack French's family later moved from the stip at Berney Arms and occupied the Lockgate marsh house until 1953.

The mill remained derelict and the sails were blown down in 1953. A temporary aluminium cap was fitted in 1985.

In November 1988 the mill and the derelict marsh house, still owned by the Banham family, went up for sale and was bought by Mr Kim Baker for £16,000. When the marsh house was part demolished, a Mr Rod Clark, whose father once owned the Langley Mill, obtained some of these Suffolk white bricks and used them to build a fireplace at his home. He put a plaque up over the fireplace to say where the bricks came from.

MRS DOROTHY HANTON REMEMBERS:-
Dorothy Hanton, nee Carter, is the only daughter of Emma and Leonard Carter. When she left school in 1931, aged 14, her family moved to the Marsh house near to Lockgate Mill, where her father worked the mill. The marsh house had two bedrooms upstairs and two living rooms downstairs. The kitchen was built separate

and you had to go outside to get to it. It also had a dairy. There was no electricity so they used a primus stove for boiling the kettle, and candles, Tilley lamps and Mantle lamps for light. Cooking was done with a coal-fired cooking range. Water was obtained from the roof and collected in tanks, and washing was done in a copper.

Leonard had a boat called 'Chloe' and when they needed to buy coal or chicken feed he would row to Yarmouth quayside to collect it. Because of the mud-flats on the Breydon near their marsh house he would often have to sit and wait in the boat until high tide before he could get home.

They kept pigs, ducks and had about three or four hundred chickens. They would take eggs and sometimes chickens, ready plucked and dressed, to sell to the shops in Yarmouth. Dorothy would bike up the railway line to Yarmouth to go shopping or to deliver eggs.

Dorothy lived with, and worked for, her parents until World War 11 when she went to Cambridge to work in a factory for the war effort. When she returned home, a few years after the war had finished, her parents had moved to a Fred High's old marsh house by the Halvergate Fleet, close to High's Mill, and her father now kept cattle.

Dorothy remembers being Temporary Postmistress at Berney Arms when Violet Mace took a holiday. Eliza Hewitt lived in the other Station cottage at that time and would bring her regular cups of tea. Dorothy also delivered the post at Berney for a short time and when 'Yoiton' was the postman she would do the postround on 'Derby' day so 'Yoiton' could go to the races.

Dorothy married Maurice Hanton in 1959. Maurice worked for a time for Stanley Hewitt at Raven Hall and for 'Yoiton' at Ashtree Farm. Shortly after they married they moved away, in 1960, and High's old marsh house which had holes in the walls soon fell down.

WORLD WAR 11.

During World War Two many of the men working on the land were in reserved occupations but several of the younger men and women were called upon to help the war effort. Violet Hewitt joined the WRAF, aunt Ruth went into the ATS while Dorothy Carter went to Cambridge and mother, Ellen, went to Welwyn Garden City to work in a factory.

Two war casualties from the 'strip' were:
Arthur James Hewitt, son of 'Long' Jimmy and 'Lady' Rose Hewitt, who was in the army and died 24 January 1942 on active service. He lived at number 4 cottage, and,
Robert Farrow, the son of Jack and Florrie Farrow of number 1 cottage. He too was in the army and died during the war. His memorial is at Cantley.

According to Bob Mace there are two bomb craters on the marshes on the Yarmouth side of the Berney Arms public house and one crater on 'seventeen acre' marsh, near the strip. Ivan Mace, who lived at the Bungalow during the war years recalls shrapnel falling on the bungalow roof but fortunately none of the buildings were seriously damaged and no one was injured.

Evacuees from Yarmouth often came to stay overnight and lodged in some of the houses.

Barrage balloons were placed over Breydon to prevent enemy flying boats landing on Breydon Water, and the rivers were patrolled, first by the navy and later by the army. Joseph Williams ('Paddy') who was in the army spent some time on the river patrols.

I remember my nanny telling me that when she was living at Raven Hall during the war years that she would often be out picking mushrooms with my mother when doodlebugs would come over making a frightening noise. She said they would drop their mushroom baskets and run for cover.

The Yarmouth Mercury of 29th March 1947 carried the following information:

'Barbed wire which was used as a defence during the war on the Conge, Great Yarmouth would be removed, compressed into bales, to be sunk into the west end of Breydon on the North Wall about ten feet from the wall.'

Figure54. Railway gang circa 1920. Billy Runacles, centre and Thomas Edward Hewitt, right, were both living at Berney. Photo supplied by Sid Gibbs.

RAILWAY AND STATION HOUSES.(TG460053)

The Yarmouth and Norwich Railway was incorporated 18th. June 1842 and opened 1st. May 1844. The track runs along the north side of the Yare through Reedham and Berney Arms. A station or 'halt' was provided at Berney Arms as a result of an agreement of 6th June 1843 between the Yarmouth and Norwich Railway and Thomas Trench Berney, the landowner. Berney agreed to sell the land providing the railway company would maintain a station there in perpetuity.

In 1845 the Yarmouth and Norwich line became part of the Norfolk Railway and in 1850, as a result of a lack of passengers, they decided to no longer halt their trains at Berney Arms and argued that the original agreement in 1843 specified a station but omitted to specify that the trains should stop. A legal confrontation ensued and continued until 1860 when the company agreed to stop one train each way on Mondays, Wednesdays, and Saturdays. The railway company anticipated the outcome of the legal battle and services were in fact recommenced in 1855.

An electric telegraph was laid by the Yarmouth and Norwich Railway in 1844, the first line in the country to have block signalling Berney Arms Halt is the smallest station in England with only one platform. The platform was originally about sixty paces long but it is now only about twenty four paces. The west part, the part now in use, has been built-up with wooden sleepers and has an ash surface. In days past when steam trains had several carriages the train would pull up with the guards van at the platform and the locals would always use the carriage near the guards van. Today the trains only have two carriages and the

Figure 55. Eliza Hewitt at the back of the east station cottage. Note the fence made from railway sleepers. Photograph supplied by Ivan Mace.

Figure 56. Berney Arms station 1946 showing locals Mrs Ellen Williams with the pram, Mrs Runacles, Miss Violet Hewitt and Mrs Elsie Bailey at the carriage window. Photograph supplied by Violet Mace (nee Hewitt).

passengers have to contact the guard to request him to stop the train at Berney. He opens the door for them.

Figure 57.The station cottages in March 1969.Photograph: Peter Allard Collection.

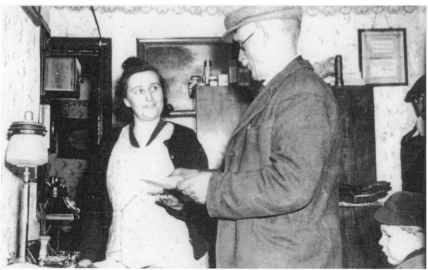

Figure 58. Henry Hewitt and Violet Mace, postmistress in her siting room at west station cottage. On the edge of the photograph is her husband Bob Mace and her son Brian Mace. Photograph supplied by Peter Allard.

67

Berney Arms : Past and Present.

An old oil lamp bearing the words 'Great Eastern Railway' was attached to the station signboard, it can be seen in figure 56. It remained at the station until a few years ago when it went missing.

There was no proper lighting on the platform until 1952 when the locals complained that it was dangerous and the railway gave in and erected some lights. The station mistress Violet Mace, or her father Albert Hewitt, would light them and refill the containers with paraffin, which would be delivered by the guard.

There was a wooden signal box, which when we lived at Berney Arms, was worked only in the summer months. It operated four signals, near and far for each direction. When Violet Mace and her father Albert Hewitt moved to the station cottages in 1947 there was an old disused wooden signal box at the side of the back garden. It had inside a copper for boiling clothes and was used as a wash-house. This old box was slightly smaller than the signal box that was in use.

During the 1950's and early 1960's there was a bell on the west station house wall outside the living room window. It was worked from the Reedham signal box to warn that the train was on it's way.

The Great Eastern Railway used the Tyer Permissive Tablet instrument between Reedham Junction and Breydon Junction without involving Berney Arms, but Tyer's one-wire, three-position block instruments were provided at Reedham, Berney Arms and Breydon Junction.

The signal box which was in use until the early 1960's was bought by Mr Manning and moved to the pub in 1964 where he used it as a storeroom. Kavan Hunt, who lived in the station cottages, had the switchgear box and kept his ferrets in it.

In the 1950's there was also a black shed standing near the signal box. It was built of sleepers and was tarred black, and was used by the railway workers as a store for their equipment.

There was also a GPO red telephone kiosk situated near the station marsh gate in the 1950's. This too was bought by Mr Manning and moved to the pub.

The station buildings were built at the same time as the railway in the 1840's and were built of red brick and slate, and were semi-detached cottages. One of the rooms in one of the cottages was used as the Post Office, rail ticket office and waiting room and there would be a blazing coalfire in the winter. Like most of the other houses in Berney they had no electricity nor running water, and had a brick cistern and barrels to catch the rainwater from the roof. In later years the Hunt family had churns of water delivered from Yarmouth by train.

When Bob and Violet Mace were at the station cottages during the 1950's their rent was 8s 9d., and they could have bought the pair of cottages for £50, but refused the offer, and later in 1956 moved to the the Island. When the Hunt family lived in the adjacent station cottage in the 1960's they too had the opportunity to buy the cottages, for £250, but also declined and moved away in 1969. Shortly afterwards the station cottages were demolished. The footings for the station buildings are still visible today but are overgrown and fenced off.

Berney Arms : Past and Present.

To the north east of the station stood a black barn. Inside on the wall was written '1934' and the name Hewitt. It is now called the 'Lodge' and is owned by the RSPB.

The post office was incorporated into the station houses and several of the locals took the job of delivering the post. They delivered to the residents of the eleven dwellings in Berney Arms and to some of the people living in the marsh houses by the Halvergate Fleet. Seven Mile House had their post delivered by the Reedham postman/woman. After the station cottages were pulled down there was only a few remaining residents and the

Figure 59. Violet Mace lighting the station lamps in 1953. Photograph supplied by Violet Mace.

postal deliveries were made from Yarmouth and a postman was sent down by train three times a week. By 1980 the deliveries were down to once a week, according to an article in the Yarmouth Mercury on 18th January 1980.

Some Occupants and Staff at Railway Cottages:

Name	Description / Notes.
Thomas Johnson	Stationmaster / Postmaster 1908
Fred Greengrass	Stationmaster / Postmaster 1916
Mr Staff	Signalman circa1928
Thomas & Eliza Hewitt family	c.1891 to 1910. Railway Platelayer / ganger (East house)
Mr & Mrs Runacles	c.1920's till 1947 She was Post & Stationmistress (West house) Mr Runacles was signalman & railway ganger. He died in1946.
Albert Hewitt & dau. Violet	He was Railway Ganger from 1947 She was Station &Postmistress (West house)
Bob and Violet Mace	Violet was Sation & Postmistress till 1956
Eliza Hewitt	1940's till 1953. Retired widow (East house)
Rose & Dick Howard	1956 She was postmistress & he worked for railway (West house)
Ralph & Elvera Hunt & family	till 1969. He worked for railway (East house)

Figure 60. The station platform in 2000.

Berney Arms : Past and Present.

Some local postmen and postwomen:

Name	Approx Date	Source
Fred Hewitt	1930's	Bob & Violet Mace
Violet Hewitt	1938 /9	Bob & Violet Mace
Millie Hewitt (High)	early 1940's	Bob & Violet Mace
Elsie Bailey	late 1940	Bob & Violet Mace
Dennis Appleton	1940's	Bob & Violet Mace
Reg Matthews	early 1950's	Bob & Violet Mace
Henry Hewitt 'Yoiton'	circa 1960	Bob & Violet Mace
Mr Hitchcock	late 1950's	Bob & Violet Mace
Dorothy Hanton	Temporary 1950's	Dorothy Hanton
Mr Arthur Best (Yarmouth)	1970 to 1980	G.Y. Mercury 18:01:1980

Figure 61. Albert Hewitt, Railway ganger, by the Berney Arms signal box circa 1953.

RAVEN HALL AND LANGLEY MILL. (TG466046)

Raven Hall stands on Langley Detached Marshes on the Island across the river Yare and opposite Berney Arms hamlet. It is thought to have been built in the seventeenth century. A building is marked on Faden's map of 1797 at this location although it is not named. On Bryant's map of 1826 it is shown as 5 Mile House and on later Ordnance Survey maps as Raven Hall.

It is built of bricks and has a thatched roof. According to Barbara Hewitt, who lived there in the 1950's, it had five bedrooms, a large kitchen, two living rooms and two other rooms with a passage to the coalshed. Outside there was a dairy and cowsheds.

'Yoiton' started his life as a marshman here and occupied Raven Hall from about 1924 till 1946.

Berney Arms : Past and Present.

My parents and I spent about a year living here when I was a small child in 1946/7, when the river froze over. I have heard the tale told that 'Yoiton's' dog Moss was sent from the Berney side to walk across the frozen river with a rope tied to its collar, to be met on the other side of the river by father who then tied the shopping list to the dogs collar. The dog then went back across the river to 'Yoiton' and nanny got our shopping when she went to Yarmouth. The dog was then sent back across the river by 'Yoiton' with a rope which was attached to the grocery box and father pulled the grocery box across the frozen river and sent the dog back with the rope.

During that freeze, on 18th. February 1947 a boat ran into ice near the Berney Arms and soon afterwards the 'Daniel-M' got stuck behind. The boat 'Futurity', coming from Norwich, where it had unloaded it's cargo of coal, succeeded in forcing a channel through the ice.

When we moved out of Raven Hall it stood empty for about a year till Stanley Hewitt moved in as the marshman in about 1949.

On the morning after the flood of 1953 Stanley and Barbara Hewitt remember that the water there was about three feet deep and their horse had gone onto a mound of earth, left behind after a dyke had been cut, to keep out of the water. Stanley had trouble trying to coax the horse down. Lots of the rabbits and hares had got on the haystack to escape the floodwaters.

The level was part of the Dashwood estate until in 1961 it became the property of Mr Askew. Stanley and his family moved out of Raven Hall, and across the river to Ashtree Farm,

Figure 62. Raven Hall with Henry, Annie and Stanley Hewitt in the 1940's. Photograph supplied by Carol Brackenbury.

Berney Arms, in 1962, and in 1969 Raven Hall was bought by a Mr Williams as a holiday home.

Bob Mace recalls that in World War Two about twenty four bombs landed on the Island and about seventeen were exploded by the army, one of these was only about 20 yards or so from Raven Hall. The bomb-crater would fill with water and the cattle would drink from it.

72

Berney Arms : Past and Present.

Langley Mill (TG466045) stands close to Raven Hall. It was shown on the 1797 map as a drainage windmill but un-named. The current mill was probably rebuilt at some time and was a redbrick tower, patent sail mill of medium height with three storeys. It drained about 300 acres at the tip of the Island.

The windmill continued to function until about 1941/2. There was also a steam engine, and in the 1940's and early 1950's a tractor engine was used to pump the these marshes.

Figure 63. Langley Detached mill circa 1948. Roy Clark has started to build a chimney on the side of the mill. Photograph supplied by Rod Clark.

The derelict mill was part of the Beauchamp estate and was bought in 1948 by Mr Roy Clark for about £25 and converted into a holiday home. It was later sold to Mr Laurence Davis, the brother of Mrs Hitchcok who had once lived at the bungalow at Berney, in about 1959. The mill was later owned by a Mr. Ingram. The present owner of the mill is a Mr. Daniel Webster.

Figure 64. Raven Hall in 2000. Photograph supplied by Stanley and Barbara Hewitt.

DR IAN GRAY REMEMBERS:-

'As a school-boy in the thirties, on boating holidays, I knew the Berney Arms merely as an old pub which marked 'landfall' after crossing Breydon Water. However, I was to make a closer acquaintance when I came to live in Reedham in 1949. The practice I joined was based upon Acle & Brundall, and Reedham, together with many adjacent villages, was part of the practice catchment area.

Living and working from the surgery in Reedham, then, I soon learned that my territory included the Berney Marshes and the inhabitants thereon. In those days they were 'populated' by several families (mainly called Hewitt or Mace) most of whom lived in farms on the North bank of the Yare. In addition there was, and is the Berney Arms pub at the confluence of the Yare and Waveney rivers.

In my time there this was a 'halt' and trains were required to stop there if the passenger so requested by informing the guard. Indeed, the train, or river, were really the only means by which one could gain access to this area. There was no road on the marshes; a Land Rover was alright in the dry weather, but only then. I believe my successor used a helicopter on one occasion but otherwise a tractor was the best 'ambulance'.

It is worth noting that, in common with many rural practices at that time, the Doctor was also the chemist. (There was no chemist between Norwich and Yarmouth.) So one made up medicines destined for the Berney Arms and handed them to the guard who would kindly drop them off at Berney Arms station where, the station-mistress, would see they were delivered. All this was done for free but, inevitably, change came and a bottle of medicine was charged at 'passenger rate'. I have it on good authority that it was not unknown for the doctor to travel on the footplate - steam train of course. I well remember that I was able to catch a train

Berney Arms : Past and Present.

down to the Berney Arms about 7-30 a.m., walk across the marsh to the appropriate farm, do my call, have the return train stopped and be back for morning surgery at nine o'clock. At other times one could cycle down the rail-side track. This was not without its hazards as I discovered at 3 a.m. one dark night when, with the wind blowing in my ears, I failed to hear the approach of the night mail and got a real fright when a gigantic locomotive roared past!

The pub produced its problems for the doctor culminating in a late evening emergency call which concluded with the Doctor, River Inspector and The Gorleston inshore Rescue Launch arriving to find the casualty soundly sleeping - a case of breakdown in communications! After this it was decided that casualties could be dealt with easier via Burgh Castle where, at least, there was a road.

I moved to the Brundall end of the practice in 1953 so lost touch with the Berney marshes, except when deputising for a partner's holiday. But one never forgets the impact that the Berney Arms and surrounding marshland made upon one. The wildlife is unique in many ways and the sheer desolation of the marshes on a cold, misty November afternoon contrasts sharply with the exuberant grazing land and hundreds of cattle fattening there in the summers of long ago.'

MR JOHN BERNEY REMEMBERS:-

Mr John Berney took over the running of the Berney Arms Marshes in about 1951.

He remembers a tale about Henry Hewitt painting the living room at Ashtree farm with green tractor paint, much to the disapproval of Henry's wife, Annie Maria. He remembers hearing Henry Hewitt on the radio and was quite amused that Henry did not stutter on the radio but did in everyday life.

On one occasion he saw Henry removing a horse from a dyke in which it had got stuck. Henry dug a slope into the dyke, put a collar on the horse and used a block and tackle to pull the animal free.

Henry told him that when he and his brothers were children they put tar on the chains on the marsh-gates and asked people to pay them to let them though. If they did not pay they got tar on themselves.

He remembers one occasion when he had come to visit Berney Arms, sitting in the station waiting room in front of a roaring fire with the wind howling outside, so loud that he did not hear the Norwich train coming and so he missed it. He borrowed a bike at the station and cycled along the track side to Reedham, once there he found a porter and asked him to put the bicycle on the next train back to Berney, and he caught the next train from Lowestoft to Norwich. Before WW1 in his great grandfathers time they used a flag to stop the trains at Berney.

He recalls Henry telling him that windpumps were better than electric pumps because electric pumps pumped too fast; faster than the flow of the water in the dykes and would need to be turned on and off all the time.

Figure 65. Raising of the sunken Lowestoft Trader near Berney Arms in May 1910. The mill in the distance is the Langley Detached Mill.

Figure 66. Langley Detached Mill in 1960.

Figure 67.

Langley Detached Mill and Ravenhall, circa 1941.
P. W. Browne

Bottle Message went to Norway

Sheila Williams of 7 Cottage, Berney Arms threw a bottle containing a message into the sea last year, and on Thursday she received a reply from a 14-year-old boy who lives in Norway. His name is Arnfinn Helgesen, and his home is on a small island near Fredrickstad.

The two are now to become regular penfriends.

An item from the Great Yarmouth Mercury 30th March 1961.

SHOCKING ACCIDENT ON THE RIVER YARE. — On Thursday afternoon a shocking accident occurred on the Yare, near the Berney Arms. A wherry, named the Emily, of Horsford, grounded on a mudbank, and the master, William Bird, threw a rope to another wherry, the Express, which happened to be passing. Bird unfortunately got his leg in a coil of rope, and the Express going at a rapid rate, having wind and tide in her favour, almost tore his foot from the limb, the bones protruded considerably from the wound. So great was the force that the rope, a new one, capable of bearing a strain of four tons, actually parted. Bird was taken on board the Express and brought to Yarmouth, where he was at once conveyed to the Hospital. In addition to a compound fracture of the leg, it was found that the ankle joint was torn completely open. On Monday the poor fellow was getting on favourably, and hopes are entertained of his recovery.

Newspaper cutting frpm July 1868.

Berney Arms : Past and Present.

BOAT ACCIDENT.

· LOSS OF THREE LIVES.

On Saturday a boat accident, attended with the loss of three lives, was reported on Breydon Water, into which the Yare falls, at Berney Arms. It appears that four smacksmen, named Alfred Peek, George Bly, Frederick Smith, and Edward Boulton, hired a small boat at Gorleston, and rowed as far as Berney Arms. There they made a stoppage of five minutes for refreshments. In returning Peek and Boulton rowed as far as the Cross Stake. A change of rowers was then proposed, and Peek, in attempting to walk aft, caused the boat to upset, and the whole of the party were thrown into the water. Smith succeeded in clinging to the boat until he was rescued, but his three companions were swept away and drowned. Their bodies had not been recovered up to a late hour yesterday.

Newspaper cutting from June 1889.

The Weather.—The frost has been unusually keen in this locality. The marshes and dykes have been much frequented by skaters during the past week, and on Christmas-day numerous individuals walked across the river from the Burgh side to the Berney Arms, a feat not often performed. The cold has been most intense.

Newspaper cutting from Decembr 1860.

Berney Arms : Past and Present.

Census Records

Berney Arms is in the parish of Reedham and the available censuses at The Norfolk Record Office and on the internet have been examined. Unfortunately full addresses were not given and I have had to deduce which were the people at Berney Arms.

1911 Census:

Seven-Mile House

Robert Joseph Burgess	51	marshfarmer	
Elizabeth Burgess	43	wife	bn. Beccles
Robert George	17	son	farm worker
Frederick James Burgess	6		

Cottages 1 to 4

John Farrow	36	marsh labourer
Florence Farrow	33	wife
Annie Farrow	10	
Dorothy Farrow	8	
John Farrow	5	
Lillian		

Cottages 1 to 4

Robert J Lake	31	marsh labourer
Eveleen B Lake	29	
Ann Banham	2	boarder

Cottages 1 to 4

James Hewitt	23	labourer
Rose Hewitt	25	
Mildred Hewitt	0	

Ashtree Farm

William Hewitt	72	marsh farmer
Susannah Hewitt	73	wife
Samuel Baldwin	15	grandson, farm worker ,bn Kent

Bungalow

Isaac J Hewitt	47	millwright	
Rose E Hewitt	56	wife	
George E Hewitt	24	son	millwright
Frederick A Hewitt	23	son	platelayer
Daisy H E Hewitt	19	dau	

Cottages 6/7

William Farrow	32	marsh labourer	
Gertrude Farrow	30	wife	
James Farrow	70	father ,	marsh labourer
Walter Farrow	2	nephew	

The Old Berney Arms Inn

Thomas Hewitt	47	platelayer	
Eliza Hewitt	42	wife	
William Thomas Hewitt	27	son	general labourer
Robert Hewitt	22	son	general labourer
Harry Hewitt	19	son	general labourer
Harriet Hewitt	17	dau	general domestic serv.
Rose Hewitt	14	dau	general domestic serv.

James Hewitt	12	
Thomas Hewitt	10	
Blanche Hewitt	8	
Gertie Hewitt	6	
Ada Hewitt	3	
Ernest Hewitt	0	
Station Cottage		
Thomas Johnson	64	signalman
Elizabeth Johnson	67	wife
Station Cottage		
Benjamin Webb	33	platelayer
Tottie Maria Webb	33	wife
Benjamin Webb	11	son
Maurice Webb	8	son

1901 Census :

Entry 186:Seven Mile House

Robert Burgess	41	Dairy Farmer	(son of George)
Elizabeth Burgess	32	wife	
Robert Burgess	7	son	
Alice Burgess	14	sister	
Harry Bedingfield	17	farm Servant	

Farmhouse Uninhabited(This is the marsh house near 7-mile where Thaxter family lived)

187: Cottage 1:

James Farrow	60	widower/marshman/cattle stockman
William Farrow	23	marsh labourer
John Farrow	26	marsh labourer (dies 1949, middle name Alfred, nickname 'Jack'.)
Florence Farrow	23	Dau-in-law/Dom housekeeper (wife to John, middle name Mary, dies Sept 1968)

188 Cottage 2:

James Farrow	28	Marsh labourer (son of above James Farrow?)	
Sarah A. Farrow	27	wife	from Burgh Castle
George R. Hewitt	6	stepson	
James W. Farrow	2		from Burgh Castle

189:Cottage 3

Edward Banham	23	marshman	from Wickhampton (son of Bob Banham of the Butterfly Mill on the Halvergate Fleet)
Mary Ann Banham	23	wife	from Chedgrave (nee Hewitt dau of King Billy)
Frances Banham	3	dau	
Grace Banham	1	dau	

190: Cottage4

81

William Patrick	32	widower/Marsh lab (nickname 'Tooshe', later at Haddiscoe Dam)
Stephen Patrick	12	son
Blanche Patrick	9	daughter (attended Berney Arms school and then Reedham school from 14-4-1902)
William Patrick	7	son (later marshman by New Cut in Raveningham Detached Parish)
Ernest Patrick	6	son
Pamela Patrick	22	sister/housekeeper. From Morley St Botolph

191:Ashtree Farm

William Hewitt	61	Dairy farmer (dies 1928, nicknamed King Billy)
Susanna Hewitt	63	wife from Gt Yarmouth (his 2nd wife, she dies 1914)
James Hewitt	19	son (middle name David, nickname 'Westmacot', later becomes the marshman at Ravenhall on the Island, and then here at Berney in 1924, dies Jan. 1968)
Eunice Hurrell	25	stepdaughter, from Gt Yarmouth

192: Bungalow

Isaac Hewitt	36	millwright (son of King Billy, dies Dec 1946)
Emma Hewitt	46	wife from Fritton (dies Dec 1932)
George Hewitt	14	son (later railway carpenter and millwright, dies Dec 1980)
Fred Hewitt	13	son
William Hewitt	11	son
Daisy Hewitt	9	daughter
Blanche Bruce	19	stepdaughter/domestic

193 Cottage 6/7

Charles Beddingfield	43	gen. Labourer
Jane Beddingfield	44	wife
Albert Beddingfield	11	son
Lilly Beddingfield	9	daughter
Harriet Beddingfield	7	daughter
Arthur Beddingfield	5	son
Annie Beddingfield	3	daughter

194:The Inn

John Andrews	45	licenced victualler
Sarah Andrews	40	wife
Robert Andrews	21	gen lab
William Andrews	18	son
Arthur Andrews	16	son
Fredrick Andrews	15	son

Ethel Andrews	13	daughter	
Lilly Andrews	11	daughter	
Elizabeth Andrews	9	daughter	
Ada Andrews	6	daughter	(attended Berney Arms

school)

Dora Andrews	3	daughter	(" " ")

195:The Station

Thomas Johnson	57	signalman
Elizabeth Johnson	56	wife

196:The Station

Thomas Hewitt	38	platelayer (son of King Billy, dies 1927)
Eliza Hewitt	33	wife (nee Banham, middle name Francis, dies

Feb 1953)

Robert Hewitt	12	(middle names Last Benjamin, dies Feb 1940)
Henry Hewitt	10	

(nickname 'Yoiton', middle name Bumbury, later marshman at Ravenhall then at
Berney Arms Ash Tree Farm, dies June 1974))

Harriet Hewitt	7	(middle name Ann, dies Sept 1975, marries her

cousin William George Benjamin Hewitt. He attended Berney Arms school then
Reedham from21-4-1902)

Rose Hewitt	5	(middle name Emma, marries 1st Sid Gibbs, 2nd

Mr Martin)

James Hewitt	3	(middle name David, drowned off HM Drifter

Fennew May 1917)

Thomas Hewitt	3mths	(middle name Fred, born 26-12-1900))

1891 Census: (April 5-6th.)
187 Nr Reedham (marsh house near 7-mile House)

James Thaxter	63	marshman
Sophie Thaxter	57	

186:Seven Mile House:

George Burgess	61	Marsh Farmer
Harriet Burgess	49	wife (previously Harriet Bullman)
Henry Burgess	20	Gen.Lab.
Alice Burgess	4	
Matilda Clarke	18	Dom.Serv.

185:Cottage 1:

Frederick Carter	43	Gen.Lab.
Louise Carter	39	wife
Leonard Carter	12	

Hilda E. Carter	10	
Frederick Carter	7	

184:Cottage 2:

James Farrow	50	Gen.Lab.
Mary A. Farrow	43	wife
James Farrow	21	Fisherman
William Farrow	12	son
May Farrow	7	

183:Cottage 3:

Robert Burgess	30	Marsh Farmer (came from 7-Mile Hs and returns there as marshman)
Elizabeth Burgess	23	wife

182:Cottage 4:

William A.Patrick	24	Gen.Lab.
Jane Patrick	34	wife (nee Hewitt, dau of King Billy)
Herbert A.Patrick	3	
Stephen Patrick	2	
Blanche Patrick	3 days	
Frances Patrick	25	sister

181:Ashtree FarmHouse:

William Hewitt	50	Marshman (King Billy)
Harriet Hewitt	49	wife (nee Pettingill, dies June1898)
Robert F.Hewitt	22	Lab.
George Hewitt	18	Lab. (later marshman at Ravenhall on the Island)
Henry A. Hewitt	15	Lab.
Mary A. Hewitt	12	dau (later marries Ted Banham)
James D. Hewitt	8	son (nickname 'Westmacott')
Harriet F. Legget	24	Gen. Serv.

180:Bungalow:

Isaac J. Hewitt	25	Journeyman Millwright
Rose E. Hewitt	35	wife
George E. Hewitt	3	son (born 7-2-1887, dies Dec 1980)
Frederick A.Hewitt	2	son (middle name Arnold, born 30-3-1888)
William R. Hewitt	1	son (born 26-7-1889)
Gertrude Bruce	9	stepdaughter
Evelyn Bruce	8	stepdaughter
Lucy Perry	15	Servant

179:Cottage 6:

George Burgess	38	Fisherman
Elizabeth Burgess	37	wife

Sarah Burgess	17	
Caroline Burgess	15	
James Burges	14	
George Burgess	12	
Mary Burgess	8	
William Burgess	6	
Benjamin Burgess	4	
Daniel Burgess	2	
Frederick Burgess	5mths.	

178:Cottage 7:

Charles Bedingfield	34	Gen.Lab.
Jane Bedingfield	35	wife
George Bedingfield	10	
Harry Bedingfield	7	(living & working at 7mile house in 1901)
Charles Bedingfield	5	(middle name Edward, in hospital in 1901,

marries Beatrice Emily Burrage, dies 1933??)

Beatrice Bedingfield	3	
Albert Bedingfield	3	
Lilly Bedingfield	1	

177:Berney Arms Inn:

Robert Thaxter	53	Publican (in 1861 a marshman in cottages, in

1851 at 7 mile House)

Elizabeth Thaxter	55	wife
Florence Fish?	20	daughter

176:Station Cottage 1:

Thomas Hewitt	29	Railway Platelayer
Eliza Hewitt	22	wife (nee Banham)
William Banham	7	son (William Thomas James Banham, born out

of wedlock, dies Oct 1923)

Robert Hewitt	2	son (dies Feb 1940)

175:Station Cottage 2:

William Edwards	61	Railway Platelayer
Harriet Edwards	62	wife
Thomas Edwards	27	Railway Signalman
Eliza Edwards	21	*Daughter-in-law*
Sidney Edwards	4	grandchild
Harriet Edwards	2	grandchild
Maude Edwards	2 mths.	grandchild

1881 Census: (April 3 -4th)
Only ten entries at Berney Arms itself so one dwelling must be unoccupied!

Berney Arms : Past and Present.

180: (marsh house near 7-mile)

James Thaxter	53	marshman	

181:Seven Mile House:

George Burgess	52	Marshman	
Robert Burgess	20	Marshman	(living at Cottages at Berney

in 1891 and returns here by 1901)

Elizabeth Burgess	17		
Abraham Burgess	13		
Henry Burgess	10		
Harriet Bullman	39	Housekeeper	(later marries George

Burgess)

182:cottage(1?):

George Chapman	23	Marsh Lab.	
Harriet Chapman	28	wife	
George Chapman	1		

183:cottage(2?):

James Farrow	40	Lab. Cement Works	
Mary Ann Farrow	34	wife	
Harriet Farrow	13		
James Farrow	11		
John Farrow	8		
William Farrow	3		

184:cottage(3?):

George Thaxter	39	Waterman	(possibly a son of John

Thaxter?)

Harriet Thaxter	68	mother	
Mary Ann Farrow	17	Dom. Servant (later marries Stephen Hewitt on	

the Island), dies 1918)

185:Farmhouse:

John Burgess	52	Marshman (at Railway cottages nr. 7-mile in	

1891)

Harriet Burgess	48	wife (at Railway cottages nr. 7-mile in	

1891)

Jane Hubbard	27	daughter	
Robert Hubbard	28	Journeyman Carpenter	
Ernest A. Hubbard	6	g'son (at Railway cottages nr. 7-mile in	

1891)

Albert R. Hubbard	5	g'son	

186:Bungalow:

Frederick Carter	32	Gen Lab.	(licensee at Berney Arms pub

circa 1886 to 1890)

Louise Carter	28	wife
Edith Carter	5	
Leonard Carter	2	

187:cottage(6?):

William Thaxter	30	Marshman
Louisa Thaxter	30	wife
William Thaxter	13	Gen. Lab.
Rosa Thaxter	10	
Almira Thaxter	8	
Percy Thaxter	7	
Herbert Thaxter	6	
Kate Thaxter	3	
Alberta Thaxter	6mths	

188:cottage(7?):

Charles Beddingfield	22	Waterman
Jane Beddingfield	23	wife
George H.Beddingfield	2mths	

189:Berney Arms Inn:

Walter Daniels	24	Licenced Vict / Farmer 25 acres
Ellen Daniels	22	wife
George Daniels	2	
Archibald Daniels	4mths	
James Blake	56	Cabinet maker - boarder

190:station cottage:

William Edwards	52	Platelayer
Harriet Edwards	53	wife
Mary A. Edwards	14	
Eliza Edwards	11	
Charlotte Edwards	9	

191:station cottage:

| George Peart | 63 | Platelayer |
| Sarah Peart | 65 | wife |

1871 Census: (April 2-3rd).
29:By the River (marsh house near 7-mile)

James Thaxter	43	marshman
Maria Thaxter	77	mother?
Maria Thaxter	43	sister
Walter Thaxter	14	nephew (middle name Joseph dies 1953, Bur Reedham)

87

Berney Arms : Past and Present.

30:Seven Mile House:

George Burgess	43	Marshman (son of James and was at Wickhampton in 1861)
Elizabeth Burgess	44	wife
Benjamin Burgess	23	Marshman
Harriet Burgess	20	
George Burgess	13	
James Burgess	11	
Robert Burgess	9	
Elizabeth Burgess	6	
Abraham Burgess	3	
Henry Burgess	11mths	
Mary A. Mallet	19	servant / dairymaid
John Page	70	visitor / labourer

31:By the River(1?):

Mary Carver	71	Cowkeeper
John Baker	45	lodger / Chelsea pensioner
William Lanham		lodger / lab.
Thomas Milligan		lodger / lab.

32:By the River(2?):

John Thaxter	57	Marshman (probably a son of Joseph Thaxter?)
Harriet Thaxter	55	wife
Harriet Thaxter	22	daughter

33:By the River(3?):

John Stubbs	55	Lab.
Elizabeth Stubbs	53	wife
Louisa Stubbs	15	
Ellen Stubbs	13	
Sarah Stubbs	11	

34:By the River(4?):

James Farrow	29	Lab.
Mary Ann Farrow	24	wife
Mary Ann Farrow	7	(marries Stephen Hewitt)
Harriet Farrow	3	
James Farrow	1	

35: Farmhouse(Ashtree?)

John Burgess	42	Marsh Farmer 63acres
Harriet Burgess	37	wife
Jane Burgess	17	(later marries Robert Hubbard)
Millicent Hanton	3	niece
Eliza Culley	28	charwoman

James Etheridge	18	servant/lab.

36:By the river (bungalow?):

Robert Bull	49	Cement maker / clay labourer
Maria Bull	43	wife
Charles Bull	17	Lab.
Maria Bull	14	
George Bull	11	
Harriet Bull	8	
Eliza Bull	6	
Emily Bull	4	
Edward Bull	2	
Eliza Bacon	52	boarder

37:By the River(6?):

James Knights	22	lab.
Caroline Knights	21	wife
George Knights	1	

38:By the River(7?):

John Green	29	Lab.
Frances Green	30	wife
Frederick Green	4	

39:Berney Arms Inn:

James Knights	44	Innkeeper (died 1876?)
Maria Knights	44	wife
Henry Knights	16	lab.
Johnathon Knights	13	(later becomes a wherryman)
Martha? Knights	8	
Eliza Knights	6	
Mary Knights	3	
Rhoda Ling	15	Gen. Servant
James Cross	45	Lodger / lab.

40: Railway Cottage:

William Edwards	42	lab.
Harriot Edwards	42	wife
Thomas Edwards	7	
Mary A. Edwards	4	
Charlotte E. Edwards	1	

41: Railway Cottage:

James Heowend?	30	lab
Charlotte Heowend?	26	wife
James Heowend?	7mths.	

1861 Census: (April 7-8th)
21: Marsh house (near 7-mile house)

James Thaxter	36	unmarrd farmer 20 acres
Maria Thaxter	67	mother/ housekeeper
Maria Thaxter	36	sister/unmarred/ dairymaid
Walter Thaxter	4	nephew

22: Marsh House (Seven Mile House):

James Burgess	65	Farmer 64 acres employs 5 men
Elizabeth Burgess	58	wife
Joseph Burgess	23	marsh lab.
Abraham Burgess	18	marsh lab.
Benjamin Burgess	13	grandson
Elizabeth High	16	dairymaid
Sarah A. Calver	12	servant- housemaid (previously at Berney cottages)

23: Cottage (No. 1 ?)

James Calver	66	Cement Lab.
Mary Calver	61	wife
George Burcham	28	lodger/ Cement lab.

   1 Unit to Let. (No. 2 Cottage?)
24: Cottage (No. 3?):

William Hanton	44	Ag.lab
Annie Hanton	49	wife
Maria Hanton	20	daughter/servant
Caroline Hanton	11	

25: Cottage (No. 4?)

John Burgess	36	Marshman (at 7-Mile House. in 1841, and at Ashtree Farm in 1871)
Harriet Burgess	31	wife
Jane Burgess	7	
Robert Thaxter	23	lodger / marshman (living at house by 7-mile in 1841, & at Berney Inn in 1891)
Elizabeth Thaxter	26	

26: Marsh House (Ashtree Farm?):

Horace Gilbert	45	Marsh farmer
Emily Gilbert	44	wife
Charles Gilbert	22	Marshfarmer
Martha Gilbert	18	Dressmaker
Fredrick Gilbert	16	
Mary Gilbert	14	

Berney Arms : Past and Present.

Sarah Gilbert	13	
Susannah Gilbert	10	
Susannah Beck	71	Mother-in-law
George Smith	17	lodger / Shepard
27: Private House (Bungalow?):		
Robert Bull	40	Lab. Cement Works
Maria Bull	32	wife
Charles Bull	7	
Maria Bull	4	
George Bull	2	
Mary Bacon	72	visitor
28: Cottage (No. 6):		
William Milligan	47	Mariner
Esther Milligan	46	wife
Sarah Milligan	11	
Thomas	9	
Elizabeth	6	
Edward	2	
29: Cottage (No. 7):		
Charles Eason	40	Lab. Cement Works
Elizabeth Eason	36	wife
30: Berney Arms Inn:		
James Knights	32	Innkeeper (from Runham)
Maria Knights	35	wife (nee Green, from Winterton)
Ellis Knights	10	
George Knights	8	
Henry Knights	6	
Johnathan Knights	3	
Ann Long	16	visitor
John Green	17	visitor/ nephew from Rollesby
Alfred Juhhall	32	visitor
31: Cottage (Station):		
George Pert	43	Platelayer E.C.Railway
Mary Pert	52	wife
Henry Pert	19	Platelayer E.C.Railway
32: Cottage (Station):		
William Booty	32	Platelayer E.C.Railway
Mary Booty	30	wife
Caroline Booty	1	

1851 Census: (March 30-31st)
3: (house near 7-mile house)

Name	Age	Description
Joseph Thaxter	65	ag.lab/marshman born at Burgh
Maria Thaxter	55	wife
James Thaxter	26	son/ ag. Lab.)twin
Maria Thaxter	26	marsh lab.)twin
Henry Thaxter	24	" " (marshman at Raven hall on Island in 1881)
George Thaxter	22	" " (a farmer in Halvergate in 1861)
Harriet Thaxter	20	
Robert Thaxter	13	grandson (at Berney cottages in 1861 & at Berney Inn in 1891)
William Thaxter	5	" "

4:Seven Mile House:

Name	Age	Description
James Burgess	53	Marshman / Ag.Lab (born at Burgh Castle)
Elizabeth Burgess	49	wife
Frederick Burgess	28	Ag.Lab
James Burgess	16	Ag.Lab.
Joseph Burgess	14	Ag.Lab
Shadrack Burgess 1	2	
Abraham Burgess	8	

5:(cottage no.1?):

Name	Age	Description
James Calver	56	Rail Lab.
Mary Calver	50	wife
Charles Calver	15	
Phoebe Clark	18	House servant

6:(cottage no.2?)

Name	Age	Description
John Calver	27	Ag Lab.
Maria Calver	25	wife
Sarah Ann Calver	2	(at 7-mile house in 1861)
Sophie Calver	1	
James Calver	1 mth.	

7:(Ashtree Farm?):

Name	Age	Description
James Duffield	63	widowed/ Marshfarmer 234 acres (born at Tunstall)
Henry Duffield	34	farmers son (born Freethorpe)
Mary Wigg	42	unmarried housekeeper
Mary Dyballs	20	dairymaid
Elizabeth Gibbs	20	housemaid
George ?	15	servant

2 houses uninhabited (cottages 3 & 4?)

Berney Arms : Past and Present.

8: (Bungalow?):

James Duffield	44	Ag. Lab.	(born Freethorpe)
Mary Ann Duffield	43	wife	(born Burgh Castle)
James Duffield	5		
Frances Duffield	1		
Daniel Duffield	3		

9:(cottage no 6?):

Joshua Clark	27	Ag.Lab
Sarah Clark	23	wife (nee Burrage)
Emily Allen	24	visitor (nee Burrage)
Margaret Burrage	56	nurse (mother to Sarah & Emily above)
Margaret Clark	1 mth.	

10:(cottage no 7?):

Abraham Gowen	27	Carpenter (born at Raven Hall on Island)
Jane Gowen	30	wife

11: (Berney Inn):

Horace Gilbert	35	Innkeeper
Emily Gilbert	35	wife
Charles Gilbert	12	
Martha Gilbert	6	
Fred Gilbert	5	
Mary Ann Gilbert	4	
Sarah A. Gilbert	3	
Mary Beck	25	unmarried dressmaker/ visitor
Eleanor Beck	21	unmarried
unnamed Gilbert 1mth	daughter	

12:(station cottage?):

Thomas Pickering	29	Rail Lab.
Sarah Pickering	25	wife
James Pickering	1	

13:(station cottage?):

George Warner	34	Rail Lab.
Emily Warner	29	wife/ dressmaker
Amelia Warner	7	
Anne A. Warner	3	
Georgiana Warner	2	

1841 Census (15th June)

It is not possible to be sure which entries are at Berney Arms but the following are likely, some having been deduced from the Tithe Apportionment.

Berney Arms : Past and Present.

This entry is probably for the marsh house next to Polkeys Mill:

Joseph Thaxter	45	marshman
Maria Thaxter	40	
Robert Thaxter	19	
James Thaxter	17	
Maria Thaxter	17	
Henry Thaxter	14	
George Thaxter	11	
Harriet Thaxter	8	
Robert Thaxter	4	(living at Berney cottages in 1861 as marshman)

The next listed entry is: (so is this another building here next to Polkey's?)

Joseph Thaxter	20	marshman (probably the son of the above Joseph!)
Ann Thaxter	20	

This entry is probably for 7-Mile House.

James Burgess	40	marshfarmer
Elizabeth Burgess	35	
John Burgess	17	(later at cottages in 1861 & Ashtree Farm in 1871 as marshman)
GeorgeBurgess	15	(later marshman in 1861 at Wickhampton)
Fred Burgess	9	
James Burgess	5	
Joseph Burgess	3	
Shadrack Burgess	1	
Susan Eliz Burgess	13	

This is probably Ashtree farmhouse:

James Duffield	50	Farmer
Caroline Duffield	20	
James Duffield	30	
Henry Duffield	25	
Francis Duffield	24	
George Duffield	20	
Mary Porter	20	servant
Ann Mingay	19	servant
Fred Mingay	20	servant

This may be the Berney Arms Inn.

Robert Rushmer	30	Innkeeper
Mary Rushmer	30	

****

LOCKGATE FARM AND LOCKGATE MILL -- FREETHORPE CENSUSES
These entries are for the Lockgate Mill marsh house and Lockgate Farm in the Detached Freethorpe Parish. It is not possible to tell from the censuses which is the farm and which is the mill marsh house.

1911
Freethorpe, Runham Vauxhall

James Banham	48,	marshfarmer, bn. Thurlton
Sarah Ann Banham	48,	wife
Benjamin Banham	17	son
William R. Banham	12	son
Letia R. Banham	6	dau.
Lucy Brett	25	dau (nee Banham)
Lucy S. A. Brett	2	grand dau
Ivy Letia Brett	0	grand dau
Leah Hopwood	14	boarder

Freethorpe, Great Yarmouth

Daniel Banham	57	marshfarmer Bn Wickhampton
Jane Banham	57	

1901
No97 Lockgate Level of Marshes Detached Portion of Parish

Daniel Banham	48	marsh farmer
Jane Banham	48	wife
William Banham	18	ag lab/ farm worker
Christiana Banham	22	dom serv
Charles King	25	boarder/ ag lab
George Watling	25	" "
? Jones?	14	nephew from Halvergate/ bricklayer/labourer

No98 Lockgate Level of Marshes Detached Portion of Parish

James Banham 39 Marshman (son of James & Ann Maria Banham who were at Upper Seven Mile House on the Detached Chedgrave Marshes on The Island)

Sarah Banham	36	wife
Lucy Banham	14	
Benjamin Banham	7	
William Banham	2	
Robert Banham	18	
Charles Garwood	5	nephew
Edward Hanton	17	lodger / railway lab.

Berney Arms : Past and Present.

1881

No. 1 marsh house

Daniel Key Banham	28	marshman	(a son of Last Banham)
Jane Anna Banham	28		(nee Smith?)
Betsy Banham	8		
Susan Mary Ann Banham	6		
Sarah Ann Banham	4		
Christiana Jane Banham	2		
Un-named Banham	5days		
Jane Banham	17		
Margaret Jones	20	sister	
Herbert Jones	1mth		
No2			
James Key	73		
Sarah Key	69		
Alice Walters?	12	granddaughter	

1871

101

Henry Thaxter	35(?)	occupation not given!
Mary Thaxter	40	
Charlotte Thaxter	9	
No 99		
George Smith	51	Marsh farmer
Mary Ann Smith	40	
Fred Smith	19	millwright
Mary Ann Smith	*11*	
Daniel? Smith	4	
William Smith	3	
Jane Thaxter	16	servant
William Pigmy	40	dom serv
Sam Clark	30	lodger / lab
Elizabeth Clark	27	
(No **98**		
Charles Forder	45	Thatcher
Rebecca Forder	42)	

1861

No 1

George Smith	41	marsh farmer

96

Mary Ann Smith	31	
Fred Smith	12	
Mary Ann Smith	6	
Sarah A. Browne	21	dairymaid
Tabitha Banham	18	housemaid (maybe daughter of Ben & Kirun

Banham then at Ashtree farm, Acle New Rd.)

No 2

James Key	53	Ag Lab
Sarah Key	52	
Daniel Key	20	
Mary Ann Key	18	
Edward Key	16	
Emily Key	12	
Jane Key	9	

1851

Only one marshman listed:

No. 22

George Smith	30	marshman / Ag. Lab.
Mary Ann Smith	22	
Fred Clark	2	

1841

Only one marshman listed:

John Withers	35	marshman
Mary Withers	35	wife
George Smith	15	
Martha Tary(?)	20	

****

INFORMATION FROM THE LANGLEY CENSUSES FOR RAVENHALL:

1911 Langley Detached

George J A Hewitt	36	marshman
Harriet F Hewitt	42	wife
Stephen V Hewitt	16	son
George J A Hewitt	11	son
Maud H F Hewitt	7	dau
David P C Hewitt	5	son

Berney Arms : Past and Present.

1901 Entry No 64a House on detached marshes near Berney Arms

George A J Hewitt	27	Marshman	(A son of 'King Billy' Hewitt)
Harriet Hewitt	33	wife	
Stephen V Hewitt	5		
Frederick W Hewitt	3		
Geo J Hewitt	11mths		

1891 (RG12/1541) Entry No 71 Marsh Level

Henry Thaxter	63	Marshman	b. Reedham
Mary Thaxter	62	wife	b. Halvergate
Charlotte Bunwell	15	dom serv.	

1881 Entry No.72   5 mile house

Henry Thaxter   52   marshman / land drainage (he was living at a marsh house near 7-mile Reedham in 1851, and was listed as a marsh labourer.)

Mary Thaxter	52	wife
Samuel Beck	45	marshman

1871 Entry No. 67   Marshes

Isaac Gowen	40	Marsh farmer
Martha Gowen	38	wife
George Gowen	6	
Ellen Gowen	5	
Emily Moore	19	servant

1861 Entry No. 63 Raven Hall

Isaac Gowen	32	marsh farmer
Martha Gowen	30	wife
Lucy Gowen	6	
Mary A. Burgess	50	Char
James Knight	14	farmer's boy/ servant

1851 Entry No59 Raven Hall

Elizabeth Gowen	50	widow farming 100(?) acres
Elizabeth Gowen	24	unmarried
Isaac Gowen	22	
Jemima Waters	27	unmarried / niece / housemaid
Rebecca Hunn	17	unmarried niece dairymaid
John Goldfinger	15	ag. Lab.

1841

Elizabeth Gowen	40	farmer
Elizabeth Gowen	10	
Isaac Gowen	13	
Rebecca Hunn	6	(niece)
Thomas Sharman	35	

| Ann Bishop | 20 | |
| Jemima Waters | 18 | (niece) |

****

BIBLIOGRAPHY & REFERENCES:

Sheila Hutchinson, The Halvergate Fleet: Past & Present, 2001, ISBN 0954168305.
Sheila Hutchinson, The Island (The Haddiscoe Island): Past & Present, 2002, ISBN 0954168313.
Sheila Hutchinson, Berney Arms Remembered, 2003, ISBN 0954168321.
Arthur C. Smith, Drainage Windmills of the Norfolk Marshes, 1990.
Robert Malster, Wherries and Waterways, 1986.
Roy Clark, Black Sailed Traders, 1961, ISBN 0715354434
A.H. Patterson, The Cruise of the Walrus, 1923.
A.H. Patterson, Hayloft to Temple, 1903.
A.H. Patterson, Wildlife on a Norfolk Estuary, 1907.
Harry Apling, Norfolk Corn Windmills, 1984.
H. W. Paar & A. Gray, The Life and Times of the Great Eastern Railway,1991.
Census Records 1841,1851,1861,1871,1881,1891,1901, 1911.
Kelly's Handbooks of Titled, Landed & Official Classes, 1889, 1925, 1937, 1962.
Kelly's Directories for Norfolk.
White's Directories for Norfolk.
Harrod's Norfolk Directory.

SOME USEFUL WEBSITES:

http://www.berneyarms.co.uk
http://www.old-maps.co.uk
http://www.wherrylines.org.uk
http://www.familysearch.org

OTHER LOCAL BOOKS BY SHEILA HUTCHINSON.

Berney Arms Remembered
The Halvergate Fleet: Past & Present
Reedham Remembered
Reedham Memories
Burgh Castle Remembered
Freethorpe Past and Present
Wickhampton Memories

Berney Arms : Past and Present.

The River Yare: Breydon & Beyond
The Lower Bure from Great Yarmouth to Upton
Halvergate & Tunstall Remembered
Cantley, Limpenhoe & Southwood Remembered
Beightom & Moulton St Mary Remembered

THE RIVER YARE:
BREYDON & BEYOND

by Sheila Hutchinson

BEIGHTON
&
MOULTON ST MARY
REMEMBERED

Sheila Hutchinson

THE LOWER BURE
FROM GREAT YARMOUTH TO UPTON

SHEILA HUTCHINSON

CANTLEY, LIMPENHOE &
SOUTHWOOD REMEMBERED

Sheila Hutchinson

HALVERGATE & TUNSTALL
REMEMBERED

Sheila Hutchinson